LOVE & GRATITUDE

THE BOOK OF FREQUENCY

CREATED BY

MULTI #1 INTERNATIONAL BESTSELLING AUTHOR & AWARD WINNING SPEAKER

ERIK SWANSON

LOVE & GRATITUDE

THE BOOK OF FREQUENCY

#1 BESTSELLER

LOVE & GRATITUDE

ERIK SWANSON

FEATURING MARIE DIAMOND

& 33 NATIONAL #1 BESTSELLERS

Quantity sales special discounts are available for corporations, associations, and other organizations with quantity purchases. For more information, please contact the publisher at the address above.

Orders from U.S. trade bookstores and wholesalers are available. Manufactured and printed in the United States of America and distributed globally by **Integrity Publishing International**.

Paperback ISBN: 978-1-964330-26-6

Hardback ISBN: 978-1-964330-27-3

Global Speakers Mastermind & Habitude Warrior Masterminds

Join us and become a member of our tribe! Our Global Speakers Mastermind is a virtual group of amazing thinkers and leaders who meet twice a month. Sessions are designed to be 'to the point' and focused while sharing fantastic techniques to grow your mindset as well as your pocketbooks. We also include famous guest speaker spots for our private Masterclasses. We also designate certain sessions for our members to mastermind with each other & and counsel on the topics discussed in our previous Masterclasses. It's time for you to join a tribe who truly cares about **YOU** and your future and start surrounding yourself with the famous leaders and mentors of our time. It is time for you to up-level your life, businesses, and relationships.

For more information to check out our Masterminds:
Team@HabitudeWarrior.com
www.DecideToBeAwesome.com

BECOME AN INTERNATIONAL
#1 BESTSELLING AUTHOR & SPEAKER

Habitude Warrior International has been highlighting award-winning Speakers and #1 Bestselling Authors for over 25 years. They know what it takes to become #1 in your field and how to get the best exposure around the world. If you have ever considered giving yourself the GIFT of becoming a well-known Speaker and a fantastically well known #1 Best-Selling Author, then you should email their team right away to find out more information in how you can become involved. They have the best of the best when it comes to resources in achieving the bestselling status in your particular field. Start surrounding yourself with the N.Y. Times Bestsellers of our time and start seeing your dreams become reality!

For more information to become a #1 Bestselling Author & Speaker on our Habitude Warrior Conferences Please text the word AUTHORS to 619-304-6268 And also go to: www.DecideToBeAwesome.com

CONTENTS

LOVE & GRATITUDE

THE BOOK OF FREQUENCY

LOVE & GRATITUDE

INTRODUCTION

THE BOOK OF FREQUENCY

A TRANSFORMATIONAL SERIES ON THE VIBRATIONS THAT SHAPE OUR LIVES

Congratulations on your decision to join us with *The Book of Frequency*—a transformational journey and series that dives into the powerful vibrations that shape our human experience. Everything in life is energy, and that energy carries a frequency. What we think, feel, and believe sends out waves that either attract or repel the people, opportunities, and outcomes we encounter. This series was born out of a desire to help readers understand, access, and align with the highest vibrational forces in the universe. Such forces empower us to live more meaningful, abundant, and joyful lives.

Each volume of this series explores two distinct but interwoven frequencies. These frequencies are not just concepts—they are forces you can activate, amplify, and align with to change your life profoundly. Through powerful stories, personal lessons, and practical applications, our contributing authors open their hearts and share how these frequencies have shaped their journeys—and how they can transform yours.

VOLUME 1 ~ LOVE & GRATITUDE

"Gratitude unlocks the fullness of life.
Love is the highest frequency of all."
~ Melody Beattie

We begin the series with the foundational frequencies: *Love and Gratitude*—the two most elevating forces of human connection and inner peace.

Living a life on purpose requires more than effort—it involves alignment. The frequencies of Love and Gratitude tune our minds and hearts to see the good, give generously, lead compassionately, and rise above fear. They are the gateway frequencies to a life of meaning and joy.

In this volume, our authors reflect on how the frequencies of love and gratitude help humans connect, forgive, and grow. Whether overcoming pain, building relationships, or stepping into their true selves, they demonstrate how Love and Gratitude are not just feelings—they are choices, disciplines, and vibrations that we can embody daily.

Let these stories show you how to survive and thrive through Love and Gratitude. Let them remind you that when you operate from a grateful heart and a loving spirit, you transform your life and elevate everyone around you.

VOLUME 2 ~ ENERGY & HEALING

"Where focus goes, energy flows.
And where energy flows, healing begins."
~ Tony Robbins

The second volume invites you to tap into two extraordinary forces that fuel our transformation: **Energy and Healing**.

Energy is more than physical stamina—it's the essence of confidence, resilience, and intention. Healing is more than recovery—it's the reclamation of wholeness. Together, these frequencies form the core of personal renewal and growth.

In this volume, many of our authors share deeply moving stories about their inner battles and the energetic shifts that helped them overcome them. Whether through emotional, mental, physical, or spiritual healing, their stories test what's possible when we believe in ourselves and trust the restoration process. Some of our authors chose to write about how they tapped into the frequency of energy to uplift themselves and those around them, embarking on a journey of success in their lives.

These lessons are not just about recovery; they are about rising. You'll learn practical ways to protect your energy, recover your strength, and expand your capacity for life's most significant moments. Healing is not a destination—it's a frequency you can choose to live in.

VOLUME 3 ~ MONEY & ABUNDANCE

"Abundance is not something we acquire.
It's something we tune into."
~ **Wayne Dyer**

Money and Abundance are more than material assets—they are energetic patterns. When you shift your frequency, you move what flows into your life.

This volume explores the often misunderstood but crucial frequencies of *Money and Abundance*. So many of us have been taught that money is hard to get or that abundance is reserved for the few. But what if these were limiting beliefs? What if money, like everything else, responded to your frequency?

Our authors will show you how to let go of scarcity thinking and embrace the flow of abundance. We will teach you how to identify your money blocks, raise your wealth frequency, and create financial and spiritual prosperity. This is not just about making money—it's about becoming someone who naturally attracts it.

From business breakthroughs to mindset shifts, this book contains real-life stories and strategies to help you align with the abundance you deserve—and live in the overflow.

A NOTE FROM OUR SERIES CREATOR
ERIK SWANSON

This series was created with one intention: to help you **raise your frequency and elevate your life.** Whether you read one volume or all three, you will find truth, tools, and transformation within these pages.

Each frequency is a choice—you become a more powerful version of yourself with every option. As you read these stories, reflect on the frequencies you're currently operating in… and which ones you are ready to rise into.

We invite you to read slowly. Reflect deeply. And most importantly, *live intentionally!* "NDSO!" No Drama - Serve Others!

With love, energy, and abundance,

~ **Erik Swanson & the Habitude Warrior International Team**

LOVE & GRATITUDE

ERIK SWANSON

TUNE IN OR MISS OUT: THE FREQUENCY OF LOVE & GRATITUDE

"Love is the beginning of the journey, its end, and the journey itself."
~ **Deepak Chopra**

Let's start with this: Have you ever walked into a room and instantly felt the energy shift? You didn't hear a word, but you *felt* it. Maybe it was electric. Maybe it was tense. Either way, something invisible was speaking to you louder than any voice. That, my friends, is frequency.

And here's the kicker—most people aren't even aware it's happening. They walk through life talking, texting, emailing, but not tuning in. Not dialing in to the frequencies around them. That's why I'm here to tell you: If you want to build real, authentic, wildly successful relationships—personal, professional, all of it—you've got to learn how to hear, feel, and *match* frequencies.

WHAT IS FREQUENCY, REALLY?

Let's get this out of the way: I'm not talking about radio towers or Wi-Fi signals (although that's a pretty cool analogy). I'm talking about the *vibes* people put out—their emotional and energetic states. Think of every person as a radio station. They're constantly broadcasting—their attitude, intentions, thoughts, emotions, all of it—on a particular frequency. And just like a radio, if you're not tuned to the right station, all you're going to hear is static.

That's why communication breaks down. That's why some meetings go nowhere. That's why you clash with that one co-worker or miss connecting with your spouse. You're on different frequencies.

THE FIVE CORE FREQUENCIES OF HUMAN CONNECTION—THE HABITUDE WARRIOR WAY

Over my years of speaking, coaching, and working with high-achievers and everyday champions alike, I've come to identify five core frequencies people operate on in conversation and connection. These aren't rigid boxes—people can bounce between them—but learning to recognize them is the first step to mastering the art of connection.

1. The Logic Frequency (Head-Based Thinkers)

These are the thinkers, the planners, and the data-driven decision-makers. They speak in facts, figures, and frameworks.

If you come at them with wild emotion or abstract ideas, you'll lose them in seconds.

How to Connect: Speak their language. Show your reasoning. Present your ideas in logical steps. Bullet points are your friend here. Don't expect them to "feel" your vision. Help them *understand* it.

2. The Emotional Frequency (Heart-Based Connectors)

These folks feel first and think later. They care about stories, impact, and how people feel. If you're trying to sell an idea or build a relationship with someone on this frequency, you need to connect emotionally first.

How to Connect: Share stories. Be vulnerable. Show passion. Make it real; make it human. Don't just give them the "what." Give them the "why it matters."

3. The Action Frequency (Doers & Drivers)

These are the go-getters. Fast-paced. Results-oriented. They don't want the backstory—they want the next step. These are your "cut to the chase" people.

How to Connect: Be direct. Be concise. Focus on outcomes. Respect their time. If you can't show them how your idea leads to results, they're moving on.

4. The Visionary Frequency (Big Picture Dreamers)

These are the "what if" thinkers. Creative. Abstract. Future-focused. They're excited by ideas that expand possibilities and challenge the status quo.

How to Connect: Speak in potential. Use metaphors, paint pictures. Give them room to dream and co-create. Don't box them in with too many details too early—they want to play in the idea space first.

5. The Harmony Frequency (Peacekeepers & Listeners)

These are the empathetic bridge-builders. They value relationships, balance, and collaboration. They often speak less, but they listen more deeply than anyone.

How to Connect: Create space. Show you care about unity. Be kind, respectful, and inclusive in your tone. Pushiness turns them off—collaboration draws them in.

HOW TO IDENTIFY SOMEONE'S FREQUENCY

Now that you've got the core frequencies, here's the real power move: *spotting them in the wild.*

Start paying attention to how people speak. Do they lead with feelings? Facts? Big ideas? Do they rush to action or ask how people are feeling about the idea?

Body language matters, too. Fast-paced talkers often signal Action. Reflective pause-takers tend to be Harmony or Emotional. Detail-heavy talkers? Probably Logic.

And, remember: people *shift*. A Logic thinker might slip into Emotional frequency during a tough personal season. A Visionary might become Action-oriented under pressure. Your job is to tune in and *adjust*.

FREQUENCY MATCHING: THE ULTIMATE RAPPORT BUILDER

Think of this like dancing. If someone's grooving to a slow jazz tune and you come in doing the Macarena, it's awkward. But when you find their rhythm—when you match their energy, tempo, tone—suddenly, you're in sync.

This is called *frequency matching*. When I worked with my main mentor, Brian Tracy, and traveled the world, we used to call it *mirroring and matching*. To be clear, it's not about faking or manipulating. It's about *respecting* the person's mode of communication. When someone feels seen and heard in their own language, they open up. They trust. And that, my friend, is the golden key to real connections and the start of the frequencies of love and gratitude.

Here are a few ways to match frequency:

- **Mirror tone and pace** without mimicking. If they're calm, slow down. If they're enthusiastic, bring energy.

- **Use their language**—repeat keywords they use, reflect their framework.

- **Ask questions in their style**—analytical for Logic, feeling-based for Emotional, and vision-based for Visionaries.

- **Adjust your outcome goal**—with Action types, focus on execution; with Harmony types, focus on relationship quality.

WHY MOST RELATIONSHIPS STRUGGLE & HOW TO FIX IT IN THE HABITUDE WARRIOR WAY

Here's the hard truth: Most relationship breakdowns aren't about *content*. They're about *frequency misalignment*.

It's not that your spouse doesn't care. It's that you're talking Logic when they need Emotion. It's not that your business partner lacks ambition. You're on Visionary, and they're on Action—and you're both frustrated thinking the other person "doesn't get it."

When we expect people to tune to our station without checking what they're broadcasting, we miss the mark.

The solution? Flex your frequency.

Start every interaction with curiosity: "What frequency is this person operating on right now?" Then meet them there. Trust me—this alone can save marriages, close deals, and turn strangers into lifelong allies... as long as you do it with love and gratitude.

RAISING YOUR OWN FREQUENCY:
BECOME A BEACON

While matching others is key, let's not forget the other side of the coin: *your own broadcast.* Are you sending out positivity, openness, and growth? Or are you sending out frustration, impatience, and defensiveness?

People don't respond just to words—they respond to the *energy behind the words.* That's why two people can say the same thing and get totally different results. I have a motto I say to myself each and every morning, which creates my own frequency: YOU NEED TO "PEA" every day—be Positive, Energetic, and Awesome!

Want to attract high-frequency people? Be one. Here's how:

- **Start your day with intention.** Your frequency is shaped in the first minutes of the day. Choose gratitude. Choose love. Choose purpose.

- **Clear your static.** Resentments, stress, negativity—it all creates interference. Let go. Breathe. Meditate. Move your body. Use my "Breathe 33 Technique" that I'm pretty well known for all around the world.

- **Fuel your mind.** Read. Listen. Learn. High-frequency input = high-frequency output.

- **Surround yourself wisely.** Frequency is contagious. Be around uplifters, not downdraggers.

- **Serve.** Nothing raises your frequency like lifting someone else's.

CASE STUDY: THE MILLION-DOLLAR CONVERSATION

Let me tell you about a client—let's call her Lisa. She was a brilliant entrepreneur with a killer product and rock-solid pitch, but she kept losing investors at the table. She'd walk out of meetings shaking her head, saying, "Why don't they see the value?"

So, I sat in on one, and I saw it right away. Lisa was broadcasting on Visionary frequency—passion, possibility, future-state magic. But her investors? Logic and Action. They wanted numbers, frameworks, and proof.

I coached her to match frequency. She opened the next meeting with a two-minute passion story (Visionary), then flipped right into KPIs, ROI projections, and execution timeline (Logic + Action). They leaned in. They signed on.

That's the power of frequency.

BRINGING IT ALL TOGETHER: FREQUENCY AS A DAILY PRACTICE

This isn't a one-time trick. It's a lifestyle. A daily, moment-to-moment discipline of awareness, empathy, and adaptability.

Start each day asking:

- What frequency am I on right now?
- What frequency would I like to be on?
- What frequency will serve me and my awesome world today?
- What frequency does this person need from me right now?
- How can I match or elevate the energy?

And remember—the goal isn't to manipulate. It's to *meet people where they are* and invite them into deeper, richer, more connected communication.

When you live like this, like a Habitude Warrior, everything changes.

You'll notice fewer misunderstandings, more collaboration, stronger partnerships, and yes, even more abundance. Because when you align your frequency with those around you—and then raise it—you become magnetic. You become a force.

And that, my friend, is where the magic happens.

DIAL IN, LEVEL UP, & BECOME A HABITUDE WARRIOR IN YOUR LIFE!

We're all walking antennas. Transmitting and receiving. All day, every day.

The question is: Are you conscious of it?

If you are, if you learn to *dial in*, to *tune to others*, and to *broadcast your highest self*, you'll become unstoppable—in business, in love, in life.

So go ahead—raise your frequency. Match it. Play with it. Master it.

And watch as the world begins to respond like never before. Become the loving and grateful Habitude Warrior!

ERIK SWANSON

As an Award-Winning International Keynote Speaker and Multi-Time #1 International Bestselling Author, Erik Swanson is in great demand around the world! He speaks to an average of more than one million people per year. Mr. Swanson has the honor of having been invited to speak to many schools around the world, including the prestigious Harvard University. He is also a recurring faculty member of CEO Space International and an alumni keynote speaker at Vistage Executive Coaching. Mr. Swanson is also the recipient of the 2024 International Book Impact Award and the United States Presidential Lifetime Achievement Award presented by the White House in 2024 for his ongoing community service and philanthropy work. Erik's speeches can be found on Amazon Prime TV, as well as on

TED Talks, where he has contributed his speeches titled, "A Dose of Awesome" and "NDSO ~ No Drama, Serve Others."

Erik got his start in the self-development world by mentoring directly under Brian Tracy. Quickly climbing to become the top trainer around the world from a group of over 250 handpicked coaches, Erik started to surround himself with the best of the best and very quickly started to be invited to speak on stages alongside such greats as Jim Rohn, Bob Proctor, Les Brown, Sharon Lechter, Jack Canfield, Lisa Nichols, and Joe Dispenza —just to name a few. Erik has created and developed the super-popular Habitude Warrior Conferences and Speaker Hearts Mastermind & Retreats, which have a two-year waiting list and feature thirty-three top-named speakers from around the world. They are "TED Talk" style events which have quickly climbed to the top ten events not to miss in the United States! He is the creator, founder, and CEO of the Habitude Warrior Mastermind, Global Speakers Mastermind, and Cafe Mastermind. He is also the creator and publisher of many book series, such as *The 13 Steps To Riches* book series, as well as *The Principles of David & Goliath* book series. His motto is clear: "NDSO!" No Drama – Serve Others!

www.SpeakerErikSwanson.com

MARIE DIAMOND

STAYING IN TUNE TO THE DIVINE SYMPHONY

THE ENERGETIC FREQUENCY OF LOVE & GRATITUDE

In the grand symphony of the Universe, every emotion plays a note. Amongst them all, two stand above the rest in their ability to realign us with the truth of who we are: Love and Gratitude.

These two frequencies are not just emotions but energetic gateways. They open the door to the Divine and, in turn, to our soul's purpose. When we tune into the frequency of love and gratitude, we don't just feel better—we become a magnet for the highest outcomes that life has to offer.

In this chapter, we'll explore how to activate the frequencies of love and gratitude in your life, and how this vibration can shift your relationships, your health, and even your material abundance. We'll also explore how to use the sacred tools of

Feng Shui and the Law of Attraction to maintain this frequency in both your home and energy field.

UNDERSTANDING FREQUENCY:
YOU ARE AN ENERGETIC BEING

Everything in the Universe is energy. You are not simply a body made of flesh and bone but rather an energy field, constantly transmitting and receiving vibrations.

Science confirms what mystics have known for centuries: emotions carry frequencies, and they can be measured in Hertz, just like sound. According to the work of Dr. David Hawkins in *Power vs. Force*, negative emotions like shame and guilt vibrate at a very low frequency (20–30 Hz), whilst love vibrates at 500 Hz and above, and gratitude at 540 Hz and above.

When your mind is stuck in thoughts of fear, anger, or resentment, your entire energy field begins to contract. This, in turn, means that your relationships become strained, your aura dims, and opportunities seem to pass right by you.

However, when you elevate your vibration by actively practicing love and gratitude, your energy field expands. You shine! You attract abundance and good fortune, and your whole life appears to radiate.

LOVE AS A COSMIC FORCE

Love is more than just a romantic emotion—it's the very fabric of the Universe. When you tune into the frequency of love, you become aligned with the Source itself. You begin to see through the eyes of compassion, respond with patience, and act with kindness.

But love isn't always easy. To love in this world, especially when you've experienced betrayal, loss, or deep-rooted trauma, requires great courage. To love, in spite of whatever life may have thrown at you, puts you on the path to true liberation.

Practice: Start each morning by placing your hand on your heart and saying aloud: "I am love. I radiate love. I receive love." This simple act recalibrates your frequency before you begin your day.

GRATITUDE: THE AMPLIFIER OF ALL BLESSINGS

Gratitude is love in action. It's the sacred acknowledgment of the gifts already present in your life. It's not dependent on having more, but on seeing more clearly what you already have.

Gratitude is a master frequency because it turns whatever you have into enough, and whatever is enough into abundance.

You may have noticed this in your own life. When you focus on what's missing in your life, or what you don't have, life seems lacking. Nothing seems to be good enough, and you find it difficult to be thankful for anything. However, when you begin to bless what you have, suddenly the world seems so much brighter! Doors open, synchronicities occur, and the impossible seems perfectly within your reach. You are lifted from limitation into expansion.

I once worked with a client who was desperate to leave her corporate job and start her own healing practice. She was stuck, frustrated, and filled with anxiety, and so I asked her to spend five minutes every evening writing down ten things she was grateful for within her current job.

At first, she resisted. "There's nothing to be grateful for!" she exclaimed, rolling her eyes. But within a week, her vibration changed. She noted that her coworkers became more supportive, and the prospect of heading off to work each morning no longer filled her with dread. Unexpectedly, she was offered a generous severance package, allowing her to transition into her dream work with financial security.

Gratitude shifts reality because it tells the Universe, "I recognize the blessing," and when you recognize blessings, more come. Think of it like this: Imagine you're giving two different people a gift. The first person responds with a big sigh, "That's not really what I wanted. My friend got something much nicer, but I guess I should get used to never getting anything I want."

The second person, however, responds, "Thank you so much! This is so thoughtful of you, and this has really brightened up my day!" Which one are you more likely to give another gift to in the future?

CREATING A FREQUENCY FIELD IN YOUR HOME

Your outer environment mirrors your inner vibration. That's why, in my latest bestselling book, *Your Home is a Vision Board*, I teach that everything within your home can either support or suppress your frequency.

To maintain the vibration of love and gratitude in your life, you must also represent it in your space.

1. Cleanse with Intention

Stagnant energy can accumulate in physical form (clutter, dust, stale air) and gradually lower your vibrational field over time. Make an effort to clean your home with cleaning products infused with lavender essential oil to cleanse the air both physically and energetically. As you do, say aloud, "I release all energy that is not of love and gratitude. I welcome only joy, harmony, and light."

2. Use Affirmations as Décor

Write down affirmations on pieces of paper and display them around your home where you'll regularly see them, such as by your bathroom mirror or on your closet door:

- "Love flows to me and through me."
- "My heart is open and my life is blessed."
- "I am thankful for the love that surrounds me."

These reminders help anchor your frequency, even when your mind is busy or distracted.

3. Decorate with the Diamond Quantum Colors

The Diamond Quantum Color for love is rose, and the color for celebration (and how better to show gratitude than by celebrating all you have to be grateful for?) is orange. When you use these colors, you help to attract those qualities into your life in a quick and easy way—think of it like a direct line to the Universe, stating what it is you want! Simply select rose and orange-colored objects or images to display around your home, such as pillows, candles, or paintings.

4. Activate Your Personal Relationship Direction

In Diamond Feng Shui, each person has a Personal Energy Number (a number from 1-9 based on your gender and date of birth) and a set of four compass directions associated with that Personal Energy Number. These four Personal Directions represent where the energy is most powerful for you in your home—think of these directions as the area where there's an invisible mailbox to the Universe. If you want to attract something, it's best to display a visual representation of it here to "post" the message straight to the Universe!

There are different Personal Directions for attracting success and money, good health, wisdom, personal growth, and, as focused here, love. If you don't already know where your Relationship Direction is located, you can download the Marie Diamond app to locate it in your bedroom with the Diamond Compass. Available in both the App Store and the Google Play Store, search "Marie Diamond" to download for free.

Once you've found it, place a small table or bookcase in your Relationship Direction so you can display symbols of love, such as:

- Two heart-shaped quartz crystals
- Images, photos, or artwork that feature couples kissing, embracing, or holding hands
- Items of equal size and height are paired together; for example, two vases or two candles
- A bouquet of silk roses
- Heart-shaped objects

THE DIAMOND FREQUENCY MEDITATION: LOVE & GRATITUDE

Let me share with you a practice I use every morning—a simple meditation that will help lift your entire energy field.

1. Sit quietly. Place both feet on the ground, spine straight, and palms open on your lap.

2.   Close your eyes. Take three deep breaths.

3.   Imagine a brilliant golden light pouring down from above, entering the crown of your head, and flowing into your heart.

4.   Inhale and feel your heart expanding with unconditional love for yourself, for others, for the entire world.

5.   Exhale and radiate that love out in all directions, like waves of light.

6.   Now, bring to mind three things you are grateful for. Feel the emotion of gratitude begin to build in your heart. Let it glow like a radiant sun.

7.   Repeat silently or aloud:

   - "I am grateful."

   - "I am love."

   - "I am connected to the Divine frequency of all that is good."

8.   Stay in this vibration for as long as you wish. When ready, open your eyes with a smile.

Do this every morning for twenty-one days and witness the subtle yet powerful changes that begin to unfold.

RAISING THE FREQUENCY OF YOUR RELATIONSHIPS

Love and gratitude are not just solo frequencies—they amplify when we share them. But often, relationships challenge us. We may attract partners who mirror our own wounds. Our lower vibrations of judgment, expectation, or resentment can get in the way of an authentic connection.

If you want to get out of the negativity trap, here are three quick ways to shift the vibration in your relationships:

1. Appreciation Before Criticism

Before offering feedback to a partner, child, or colleague, express three genuine appreciations. It's not manipulation; it's alignment. Once the frequency is tuned to love, the conversation becomes fertile ground for growth.

2. The 90-Second Reset

When someone upsets you, wait ninety seconds. Take some deep breaths and allow that immediate, knee-jerk emotional charge to subside. Then, ask: "How can I respond with love and gratitude?"

3. Gratitude Letters

Writing a gratitude letter requires just two simple steps. The first step is to get a pen and paper and think about who you'd like to address your letter to: God? The Universe? Particular people in your life whom you're grateful for? Yourself? Whoever it is, write their name clearly at the top.

Then, write about all the positive things in your life, big and small, and how much joy and purpose they give to you. Think about the things that make you smile, make your heart feel full, and perhaps even the things that you've already been able to manifest.

Even if there have been some challenging things going on in your life recently, try to reframe the way you think about them: Are they teaching you any valuable life lessons, or are they helping you to become a stronger, more resilient person? It's important to note that no one's ever going to physically read this letter, so use it as a chance to get as sentimental as you like!

Once you've finished your letter (and remember, there is no standard size for this letter—your letter could be a paragraph or ten pages long, and both are equally valid), sign your name on the bottom and write the date.

The second step, once you've written your letter, is to burn it. Wait until noon on a sunny day to burn it, since this time of day has the highest level of positive, life-affirming energy. Take a ceramic or heatproof bowl and place the letter inside. Use a match to light it and watch as the letter is reduced to ashes. As it burns, ask that the positivity of your letter reaches the soul of whoever may need it.

MIRACLES LIVE IN THE FIELDS OF LOVE & GRATITUDE

We live in a world hungry for high-frequency beings. When you choose love over fear, gratitude over complaint, forgiveness over bitterness, you can change the course of your entire life.

One of my students, a woman in her sixties, had lost her faith in love after a painful divorce. She came to me not looking for romance, but instead for help coming to peace with the idea that she might never find love again. Together, we began clearing her home, especially her bedroom, and realigning her inner thoughts to love—not just for a potential new partner, but for herself and life itself.

We practiced the love and gratitude meditation daily. She wrote letters of forgiveness. She placed rose quartz in her Relationship Direction and lit a pink candle each evening. Within four months, she met a kind and gentle man at a library talk. They've now been married for over five years, and they still meditate together every morning.

Love doesn't have an expiration date, and gratitude doesn't depend on perfection. All they ask is that you show up with an open heart and a willingness to believe in a better tomorrow.

Remember, you are not just living your life—you are contributing to the great energetic ocean we all share, so let your ripple be one of love. Remember, you don't have to be perfect—you simply have to allow your heart to tune in to the Divine Symphony.

MARIE DIAMOND

Marie Diamond is a globally renowned transformational teacher and energy master who has dedicated her life to helping others raise their frequency. As a featured teacher in *The Secret* and a Master in Feng Shui, she brings a unique blend of spiritual wisdom, energetic science, and practical tools to activate love and gratitude. Her teachings have touched millions worldwide, and her presence radiates the very frequencies she speaks of.

www.MarieDiamond.com

ANGÈLE LAMOTHE
MASTER YOUR ENERGY, MASTER YOUR LIFE

- -

"The Universe is responding to your vibration, and your vibration is about the way you feel."
~ Abraham Hicks

What's the true secret to abundance? It's all about the frequency of energy!

Ever wonder why some people seem to have it all—health, thriving relationships, fulfilling careers, abundance, and financial flow? What's their secret, you may ask?

The answer I'm about to share might surprise you: It's not time or hard work. It's not luck. It's energy mastery.

The core problem with working longer and harder is that time is a finite resource. Energy is infinite and limitless when we harness it!

From profound, life-changing experiences encountered recently, I've learned that true fulfillment and success come not from managing minutes on a calendar, making lists, or from how much time I actually have in a day, but rather from intentionally managing my energy. Yes, it's about energy mastery—simple, right!?

Your energy is your personal power. I often think of my energy like money in a bank account. When this bank account is full, I can spend my energy on anything I choose to engage in from a place of true joy, connection, love, and abundance, and naturally create and attract more of that in my life.

When it's depleted, everything feels harder, and I can easily fall into a state of overwhelm, and then scarcity and exhaustion can take over. And just like with money, I have learned how to harvest, protect, expand, and spend my energy on things that bring me great love and joy. This helps me avoid unnecessary energy withdrawals and burnout.

Through life-transforming experiences and spiritual training, I have discovered that the core source of my energy mastery comes from aligning and taking care of my four bodies: the physical, the emotional, the intellectual, and the spiritual.

When I nourish and take care of all bodies with time to recharge, I fuel my energy bank and create abundance in all areas. Some of the ways I take care of my physical body include getting enough sleep and rest, maintaining proper nutrition, and engaging in regular movement and exercise.

In terms of my emotional body, I ask myself if my emotions are fueled by love, gratitude, and joy—or by fear, stress, and resentment? Do I focus on things I enjoy and love? The thoughts that occupy my mental space are important because what I focus on grows!

Lastly, is my spirit aligned with my values, purpose, and higher self? Everything is energy. The universe doesn't speak in words —it speaks and responds to vibrations.

In each case, energy can be expanded and regularly renewed by establishing specific rituals—behaviors that are intentionally practiced and precisely scheduled, with the goal of making them unconscious and automatic as quickly as possible. To recharge, you need to recognize the costs of energy-depleting behaviors and then take responsibility for changing them, regardless of the circumstances you're facing. When we are able to take more control of our thoughts and emotions, we can improve the quality of our energy, regardless of the external pressures we face.

While it's often facilitated by practices like meditation or mindfulness, it transcends any single activity. Frequency embodies a state of being—an attitude of awareness and observation that influences how we interact with our thoughts, feelings, and environments, and, in return, how the universe interacts with us.

When your thoughts, feelings, and actions resonate with gratitude, compassion, and love, you become a magnet for more of the same in your life. Just like tuning into a radio station, the clearer and higher your vibration, the more aligned opportunities, people, and experiences show up everywhere in your life. These are synchronous and intentional and not left to chance. Implementing energy management strategies in your life will help you channel more of your energy toward your desired goals in every category to maximize abundance, especially the high energies of love and gratitude.

The most successful and happiest people on the planet have learned to master their energies. They are intentional about their thoughts, feelings, words, the activities they engage in, the people they surround themselves with, and their chosen practices. The universe communicates through signs and synchronicities to guide us toward what we need. Dedicate today to acts of kindness, love, and gratitude. When you vibrate at a frequency of abundance, you're primed to manifest your desires more quickly.

Express gratitude not only for what you receive, but also for what you can give and for the challenges that helped you grow.

As you consistently practice gratitude as a way of life, your brain begins to reframe situations. It doesn't happen overnight, but with time, you start to train yourself to find the beauty in everything and to appreciate the growth that comes from challenges. It doesn't change the facts, but it changes how you experience them.

Love and gratitude are two of the highest frequencies. Research shows that gratitude is the single most powerful way to increase happiness and fulfillment. This simple practice has propelled me forward in ways I could have never imagined.

Gratitude rewires the brain. It shifts your perception, increases happiness, and naturally raises your frequency. Through my son's health challenges, gratitude became a part of my moment-to-moment practice as I watched how life rearranged in my favor amidst the very difficult hardships. Thankfulness didn't change the facts, but its transformative power changed how I experienced them and actively chose to see the gifts and exponential growth that came from it.

The most loving, abundant, and joyful people on the planet don't leave their energy to chance. They continuously work at harnessing their thoughts and consciously choose and align them with gratitude and love. I am now very intentional about who I surround myself with and consciously choose uplifting, like-minded people in my life. I take time for rest, to re-energize, and to connect with my intentions and purpose. I am intentional in everything because I am the creator of my reality. Your outer world is a reflection of your inner world. Master your energy and you master your life.

The universe is bringing you everything you are asking for, whether you want it or not. When you shift your energy, you shift your reality.

So, ask yourself: What's draining your energy? Energy leaks result in a loss of power. You are one hundred percent responsible for your energy and for what you attract back in your life! How incredible is it to have that power to self-regulate and act as the foundation for profound change in your life? You have the ultimate power to create exactly the reality you desire!

You are responsible for everything in life, including results for your health successes, income, fitness, and relationships! When we say "yes" to something we really mean "no" to, we're expending energy on something that's draining. This causes an energy "leak" in our system, and we end up running low on fuel.

Learning to offer up a polite and respectful "no" to anything we don't feel a "hell yes" for is one of the healthiest ways to manage our energy.

What fills your energy bank account? Unconscious habits, unresolved emotions, or poor boundaries can drain our vitality. Reclaiming your power begins with recognizing where your energy is flowing and consciously redirecting it so that your thoughts align with the life you want to create.

Awareness and the power of choice lead to empowerment and responsibility. This isn't a burden; it's an opportunity and a privilege! It's power and true freedom at its core to choose and reshape anything that's not working in your life from an empowered space of radical ownership and energetic alignment. Take time to nourish your energy bank because you are one hundred percent responsible for your energy and what you attract back into your life.

Gratitude and love are not random; they come from vibrational alignment and intentional action. They have the power to transform everything and everyone; they have transformed my reality in ways I never thought possible. Let them transform the frequency of your energy for a meaningful and purposeful life!

ANGÈLE LAMOTHE

Angèle Lamothe is a high-vibrational leader who lives a heart-centered life and whose mission is to help raise the consciousness of our planet and transform the world. She is a mom of three, a triathlete, an author, and an empowerment coach who works with high-performing leaders to help them create abundance and develop their intuition, enabling them to live their richest life.

Angèle works in an acute care hospital and is obsessed with people's transformational journeys and how the power of the mind, when aligned with purpose and action, creates miracles.

Angèle leads a high-performance lifestyle and has the joy, energy, and time to do things she deeply enjoys. She can support you in developing tools to help you connect with your intuition and unleash your full power within so that you can lead a balanced and abundant life that is full of gratitude! To find all my links, visit: *www.linktr.ee/AngeleLamothe.*

Author's Website: *www.AngeleLamotheCoaching.com*

Book Series Website: *www.TheBookOfFrequency.com*

BILL GOOD

THE GREATEST OF THESE

A TRUE STORY

"There once was a note, pure and easy,
Playing so free, like a breath rippling by
The note is eternal, I hear and it sees me."
~ The Who, "Pure and Easy"

"And now these three remain: faith, hope, and love.
But the greatest of these is love."
~ 1 Corinthians 13:13

THE SONG IS OVER

The gloom of the November Sunday morning sank deeply into my soul as I navigated the dark and unfamiliar Cleveland streets. The world seemed strange—somehow out of tune. Blackening clouds and chilling winds denied harmony to spirit and body, subduing even my two teenagers in the back seat.

As I pulled up to my in-laws' house, uncertainty lay heavy as the fog lingering on the lawn. Confusion seemed the order of the day. I had come to see my wife, who had pleaded illness rather than attend the family memorial service I had conducted for my own father the previous afternoon.

Confusion promptly yielded to pandemonium. I was met at the door by my wife's parents who, after only the briefest and coolest of greetings, quite mysteriously swept up my son and daughter and headed off for breakfast, leaving me alone with my wife at the kitchen table.

The room, suddenly silent, fairly vibrated with tension. My awkward, "How are you?" opening was met with a distant stare. Her non-answer was more than answer enough: "I want a divorce."

And just like that... life as I had known it for twenty-seven years lurched to an end. Our love song—once a rich melody sung in the sublime harmony of two hearts beating together in time—was over in a single discordant blast.

GETTING IN TUNE

I remember little of the next few days. Only the memory of stumbling like Tommy, the Who's famous "deaf, dumb, and blind boy," aimlessly through what seemed an impenetrable fog remains. Looking back, I'm sure I was living in a state of clinical depression. My clearest recollection now is of profound fear... fear that I might simply forget how to breathe. The next breath seemed terrifyingly uncertain, as if the very rhythm of life was lost to me.

And, of course, there was the fear of now being forever alone.

Fast forward to Wednesday morning. It had long been my practice to awaken early and spend the pre-dawn hours of each day in communion with a Divine Being I had come to worship and trust through dedicated prayer, study, and reflection.

That morning, as I opened my heart, the presence of this God surprisingly emerged through the isolating fog of my misery and enveloped me with a warmth and compassion that was as unquestionable as it was welcome.

Then, with certain authority and a clear promise, his voice spoke calmly, piercing the disordered distortion of the emptiness that had owned my soul for the past few days, saying, "You have no idea the blessings I have in store for you." Then, he added, "Only just be faithful."

This Presence I felt and the voice I heard were so real and so intimate that I absolutely knew them to be true. I was humbled, comforted, and completely transformed by the tangible power of an enduring love wrapping around me like a blanket.

Then, as now, I couldn't overlook the fact that the promise of "blessings" was plural. And that its fulfillment was yet forthcoming.

From that instant, my very being began to resonate at an entirely different frequency. Faith and hope rose like bright spring flowers through the final grey snow of winter as I found myself transported into a whole new awareness of joyous light and universal harmony by the magnitude and dimension of a love that no previous spiritual experience had even hinted at.

For the first time, I truly understood the Bible writer John's declaration that "God is love." And, at the same time, I could testify with him that "perfect love casts out fear." You see, in that experience, I knew the promise I heard to be perfect and true. And in the power of the love I felt in that Presence, the fog and the fear dropped away, and a world of joy and possibility opened before me. I found myself in tune with the eternal.

"There once was a note pure and easy..." The frequency of that loving note sounds as a symphony in my life today, still promising blessings yet unseen and unrealized, but never, ever questioned.

"YOU HAVE NO IDEA"

"So, how did all this play out?" you ask. "Did God make good?" Truthfully, a better question would be "Have you been faithful?" The answer is "Most certainly" to the first and "As much as possible" to the second.

Twenty years later, I can testify in all truth that the frequency of Divine Love is a constant in human life if we will but let go of worldly cynicism and open our souls to receive it. That intimate Presence I felt in that time of loss has never abandoned me. And, although there have most certainly been other times of trial, the promised blessings have sung a countermelody of rich response producing deep gratitude.

My faith (such as it is) has been met with amazing and unanticipated grace, to wit:

- A call to a second career, which led to fifteen fruitful and rewarding years in pastoral ministry.

- A love affair and marriage to a captivating younger woman, which produced a delightful baby girl, now almost fourteen years old at this writing.

- A charming cabin in the wooded mountains of Northern Arizona, where the frequency of love sounds clearly, and which became my full-time home upon my retirement two years ago.

- Two friends who have walked by my side without fail through all that life has brought—the good, the bad, and the ugly—for fifty years.

- The birth of a granddaughter sixteen months ago and the opportunity to spend each Thursday experiencing a whole new dimension of love with her.

- A community of committed and talented friends who have encouraged and supported my third career—as a spiritual guide, writer, and speaker.

And the song goes on…

> *"There once was a note pure and easy.*
> *Playing so free, like a breath rippling by.*
> *The note is eternal, I hear and it sees me. . ."*

This note is played in the everlasting harmony of the Creator's love. Spoken as they were in that frequency, those first words of God to me out of the dissonance of fear and loss have become undeniably true: *I had no idea the blessings he had in store for me…*

CODA

"And now these three remain: faith, hope, and love. But the greatest of these is love."

Please understand, I didn't write this story down for me. After all, I've already lived it. I wrote it in the frequency of love and the urgency of the Divine Spirit for YOU! And it remains my most fervent wish that those of you who have walked with me this far through my story will find encouragement here for your own—wherever this finds you today. Based on my experience, I suspect that you may not be aware of the blessings in store for you.

BILL GOOD

Bill Good is a Speaker, Teacher, Bestselling Author, and Counselor. Bill Good is passionate about implementing world change through personal transformation and relationship recovery. He is dedicated to creating a pathway to healing and leading beyond the ordinary to living a life without limits. Bill holds a Master of Divinity degree from Fuller Seminary and is retired from Pastoral Ministry. He currently teaches at Grand Canyon University. He also received advanced certifications in Christian Reconciliation and Peacemaking, is a Graduate of Transformational Leadership Training, and holds a Master's in Leadership.

His online ministry features spiritual and biblical resources at the Uncommon Community Facebook page. He is also the CEO and senior counselor of Path to Peace, which provides conciliation services to organizations and individuals seeking to overcome trauma. But Bill's first love is encouraging hope through his writing and speaking. Hem is a four-time Amazon Bestselling Author, as well as a Speaker Hearts and TedX speaker.

Author's Website: *www.TheGoodFactor.com*

Book Series Website: *www.TheBookOfFrequency.com*

BRIAN SWANSON

NOT A REDHEADED STEPCHILD

What is life without the power of love and being grateful for that love? There are moments in our lives where love presents itself suddenly and without expectations. Love is deep, and gratitude runs even deeper.

I was adopted at the young age of three days. The parents who raised me showed me love simply because they had to love me. After all, they paid for me. I will always be grateful for the time, the money, and the heart they shared to make me the man I am today. However, for this story, I want to put some perspective on a love that hid from me for twenty-seven years.

My story is a positive story. Many adoptees have not had or will not have the experience I have had. Stories range from "They didn't want me then, and they don't want me now" to "I was too late, they have passed on."

I have always known that I was adopted. Sometimes, I wondered what my life would have been like if I had been with my biological parents. I occasionally asked the questions most kids in my situation asked, especially when I was upset with my parents. Who are my parents? What are they like? Are they rich? Would my life be better with them?

After growing up, finishing high school, beginning college, joining the military, and finally finding my wife of now thirty-five years, I decided that when I had children, I would want to know my biological history—mostly for my kids' sake.

It took six or seven months and some help from a family friend to track down my biological mother. As it would turn out, she lived down the road—just nine miles from where my adoptive parents were living at the time. After making a call to her, she confirmed that she was my mother. She immediately came to the house. That is where the love I did not know appeared to me.

She demonstrated not only motherly love, but love for me as an individual. She welcomed me into a family that I did not know existed. She was there for every phone call. She traveled across the country for our kids' graduation. She was there for me and my family, no matter what the circumstances. She passed away in 2017. I will always be grateful for the love she showed. I could not have asked for better circumstances and support from a mother who had given me up for adoption when she was younger.

For the next ten years, my biological mom's love and support were always apparent. However, there was still a small piece missing in my journey to find my biological parents. My father remained a mystery. My mother had suppressed all but a tiny bit of information about him. There were stories my adoptive parents had gathered throughout my years of growing up, bits of information that were shared between the adoptive lawyer and my parents. I presumed that those details would become apparent when I found my mother, but they did not. She had suppressed all the memories of my conception and birth.

Luckily enough, the small amount of information I had helped me find my biological father. I entered the information into Classmates.com (an internet database of people in graduating classes). Once I entered the information, it found someone who matched the minimum amount of information I had gathered. I sent a very descriptive email to this possible match.

It took about four months for him to finally read the email. There were many reasons for the delay. He thought it was more spam, and he occasionally visited the site because he had only joined because a friend told him that he should.

As it turned out, my biological father confirmed that he is my father. All the facts that I had gathered were enough for him to reach out immediately. Within minutes of reading the email, he picked up the phone and introduced himself. We spent a great amount of time on the phone confirming everything. There was no doubt that we were related.

Once we discover our biological parents, many questions present themselves. What is my medical background? Are there heart problems? Does cancer run in the family? One fact was interesting.

When we first got together in person, he was in a little bit of shock. He always suspected that a child existed, but he pictured a redheaded little girl. As fate would have it, this man is dark-haired. Coincidentally, I married a redhead and have two redheaded children.

He loved me and my family from day one. We now visit each other on holidays and special occasions. We speak on the phone routinely. He has shared things with me from his past that he had never shared with the children he raised. It is a great relationship. He is always accepting and supportive of me. I will always be grateful for the time and love he has given me.

We have lots of things in common. My father did not have to teach me childhood things; we shared them. We share a love for giving back to our communities. We both love our families.

As I stated earlier, my story is a positive one. However, after putting this story into words, I believe it can be labeled a success story. I found my biological parents, along with four half-siblings. We have all shared memories, stories, and new adventures with our own families. The two things that have been constant are the love we share and the gratitude we have for each other. Of course, another question arises for me on occasion: What would my life be without them?

There will always be love in our lives. Do we recognize it when it appears? Will we accept it when we see it?

I am grateful for the time that I had with my adoptive parents; they passed in 2007 and 2020. They raised me to the best of their abilities. I never received what I wanted, but I certainly received what I needed. If it were not for them, I would not be the man I am today.

My dad taught me kindness for other people and a work ethic that has brought me far in my life and on the long road through entrepreneurship. My mom taught me discipline and to accept responsibility for what is mine.

Finding my biological parents was a surprise. I grew up not looking for love from another parent; I was only curious about who my mother and father were. I was lucky enough to find them and to find a love that was unexpected. They both invited me into their lives without question. To me, believing in unconditional love comes from the precedence they each set. I can say the same about my "new" brothers and sisters.

I will always have gratitude for all four of my parents. They all provided me with something I did not think I needed. I believe we all must be thankful for the love and acts of love brought into our lives. We all have room in our hearts for love; let's just make sure we make a space for gratitude, too.

Love can be expected or unexpected. It can come from the furthest regions of our lives. In my situation, looking for love to fill an empty space in my heart was not my mission. But it indeed filled a space I did not know I had. After all, how many people can say they have four parents? I had two who raised me from infancy to adulthood. And then, there were the two who conceived me, and then later in my life, they gave me the opportunity to experience their unconditional love.

If you are looking for love, be patient—it will come. Just be certain that once it finds you, you will be grateful.

BRIAN SWANSON

Brian Swanson is a dedicated entrepreneur, podcaster, bestselling author, and business owner. His specialty is within the world of learning, teaching, and business building. His experiences include working in restaurants, bars, finance, construction, as a comic bookstore owner, disc jockey, website creator, marketer, graphic editor, and owner of GalaxyFest (a popular local Pop Culture Convention). Brian has a passion for sharing his skills and experiences through writing, speaking, and co-hosting a long-running podcast, Denim and Pearls.

One topic he loves to share is his experience of searching for his biological parents. Finding them was a positive experience, and his willingness to share has helped many adoptees conquer their fears and begin their quest to find their parents. If he is not behind the computer or orchestrating an event, you can find Brian hosting or performing karaoke at numerous venues around the state any day of the week—that is, assuming he is not traveling around the world. Learn more about Brian here: *www.Facebook.com/DJWildLife* & *www.DenimAndPearlsLive.com.*

Author's Website: *www.GalaxyFest.com*
Book Series Website: *www.TheBookOfFrequency.com*

CHRISTOPHER MUSIC

THE SECRET TO THE MANIFESTATION OF DREAMS

. . . .

LOVE & GRATITUDE

"Remember, the first thing necessary is a sincere desire, concentrating your thought on one thing with singleness of purpose.

The second is visualization—SEEING YOURSELF DOING IT —imaging the object in the same way that Universal Mind imaged all of creation.

Next is faith—BELIEVING that you HAVE this thing that you want. Not that you are going to have it, mind you—but that you HAVE it.

And the last is gratitude—gratitude for this thing that you have received, gratitude for the power that enabled you to create it, gratitude for all the gifts that Mind has laid at your feet."

~ Robert Collier, The Secret of the Ages, 1926

I began my lifelong career in the financial planning profession in January 1992, after I had just left graduate school at Kent

State University with all but one final class for my MBA. Yes, I was chomping at the bit to forge out on my own to start my firm that I had planned since the summer of 1990 when I was introduced to the Charles J. Givens Organization. This was a self-help group founded by Charles Givens, a bestselling financial guru in the late 1980s and a trailblazer for modern-day financial professionals such as Dave Ramsey, Robert Kiyosaki, and Grant Cardone.

Once I was trained with his materials, I knew I wanted to be a Financial Advisor because not only did I have an aptitude for the subject, but I also loved the professional path I was on and the possibilities in serving others that could ultimately manifest.

I always knew that I needed to work for myself as an entrepreneur because I never really found any comfort in working for someone else. I attended graduate school for the next eighteen months as I prepared to launch my firm.

Upon completion of formal schooling (the final class to be completed in the summer of 1994), I had the good fortune of being mentored by a gentleman in St. Louis who was a trainer with Givens. I was able to live there for a couple of months while my then-partner Tom and I trained to deliver basic financial services to clients.

Upon my return to Columbus, Ohio, I secured a lease in an executive office suite and got to work, shoestringing the start-up the whole time. Shortly upon establishing the company, my partner quit and went back to work a 9-to-5 job. I had to work temporary services for a couple of years as I looked for a good broker-dealer that would allow me to not only build a practice but also assist me in what I needed to be successful.

I finally found First Financial Planners in the Fall of 1993 and subsequently found a niche with ministers in the state of Ohio. I became an expert on clergy finances and tailored my services to that demographic, finding fulfilment in my work.

On a cold, snowy Saturday morning in February 1994, I sat down and worked out a plan for my small practice: to build it over a certain timeframe, to a certain number of clients, with a certain amount of assets under management, and sell the practice for seven figures. I wrote it all up that day with enthusiasm and a clear objective in as much detail as possible, since I was studying the law of attraction and using it to manifest what I really wanted.

Over the next eight years, I systematically built a very successful practice, doing quarterly seminars in each major city in Ohio and implementing financial plans for a few hundred ministerial clients. The business was built with my then-spouse out of our second bedroom, while utilizing conference room locations around these cities to meet clients face-to-face. After a few years and tens of thousands of miles on my car, we were able to build a nice boutique practice and maxed out our bandwidth for two people.

In 1999, I did a continuing education course on income tax with H&R Block. During the course, I met a gentleman named Brian, who was an accountant for a local corporation. He told me that he wanted to get into financial planning as a new career. After much discussion, I told him that I would take him on under two conditions: one, that he would be required to buy me out between three and eight years from that time, and two, that he would do everything I told him to do without exception. He happily agreed, and we began to work together.

After two years of training and building up his clientele, I decided that I was going to sell at the three-year mark. I was ready for a new challenge, and Brian became an exceptional advisor. So, over the course of the next year, I wrote up every single detail I knew about each client and vendor of the practice—to the level of their pet's name, favorite candy bar, etc.—and placed it in three huge binders so that he knew everything I knew.

I introduced him to every single client and vendor, whether in person or over the phone. I then told him that if he ever had any issues with anything in the practice, he should consult those binders first before he would contact me. That seemed to work well because he only called me once due to a mistake that I had made with a client a year prior that I had to fix.

I had hired an attorney to help me draw up all the business sale documents and structure how the buyout was to occur. Over that year, all the details were ironed out and all preparations were made so the closing would go smoothly. On January 2, 2002, we met at the law office on the northwest side of town and signed the documents. There was an air of celebration and of hopeful beginnings because we sat and joked while we closed the transaction—with high fives and all!

As I drove down the road along the Olentangy River back to my house after closing, I was struck with an overwhelming epiphany, and I burst out laughing uncontrollably! As a matter of fact, I reached for the radio to try to find a song much like

Tom Cruise did in the movie *Jerry Maguire* when he signed Cush as a client and celebrated by finding the song *Free Fallin'* by Tom Petty and sang at the top of his lungs!

I had the same reaction, only I needed something harder from my mixtape! In that moment, I realized that I had sold my company in almost the exact same time frame, with almost the exact number of clients, and with almost the exact amount of assets under management, for the seven figures that I had written up and forgotten about just eight years earlier.

When I originally wrote the plan, I must have been convinced that I had already completed it! I had total faith in myself and its manifestation, and carried on day after day, visualizing the outcome, even if only in my subconscious, as it guided the way.

Most importantly, it was my gratitude for the love I had for my purpose and the ability to carry it out, for the vendors and clients, and for Brian that made me so happy to create that work of art and pass that legacy on to all of those connected with that company.

Mr. Collier got it right one hundred years ago. He really knew the secret to the manifestation of dreams! Now it's time for you to manifest yours!

CHRISTOPHER MUSIC

Christopher Music, MBA, RFC, CBEC, is a thirty-three-year veteran of the personal financial planning profession. He has owned, built, and sold two firms since 1992, resulting in the improvement of the financial destinies of thousands of families in the US. He is a Wall Street Journal/USA Today bestselling author and an award-winning international speaker on financial topics. A Certified Business Consultant, Registered Financial Consultant®, and a Certified Business Exit Consultant®, he is committed to expanding his knowledge and expertise in the fields of personal finance and economics for the ultimate benefit of small business owners.

He has shared the stage and/or collaborated on projects with Grant Cardone, Forbes Riley, Steve Forbes, Brian Tracy, Erik Swanson, Robert Allen, Rudy Giuliani, Mel Robbins, and other leading coaches and consultants. Christopher currently lives his life virtually as a digital nomad, traveling the world full-time and working with healthcare practice owners as The Professional's Prosperity Mentor. He can be reached at CM@ChristopherMusic.com.

Author's Website: *www.ChristopherMusic.com*

Book Series Website: *www.TheBookOfFrequency.com*

CLEVELAND AUZENNE

WHEN MY FREQUENCY MET MY FUTURE

WHEN MY SPIRIT KNEW BEFORE
MY EYES COULD SEE

I didn't always understand how energy worked. I knew what it meant to hustle and push through, but I didn't know that life responds not just to your actions but to your frequency.

It wasn't until I became a certified instructor in the Napoleon Hill philosophy in 2023 that the dots started to truly connect. I had always believed in hard work and integrity, but now I had language for something I'd felt my entire life. It was more than mindset. It was vibration. It was alignment.

And above all—it was gratitude.

I thank God for planting the seed early, especially through my father. He used to take us on road trips across the country. Before I hit my teenage years, I'd already seen more states than most adults ever would. We didn't know it then, but those long hours on the road were shaping us—teaching patience and presence, teaching us to sit still long enough to witness life moving, even when it felt like nothing was happening.

My dad never called it "frequency," but that's what it was. He moved in trust. He moved with calmness. He didn't let the outside noise decide the tone of the journey. As I reflect on those days now, I realize that's where I first learned this: The energy you carry is louder than the words you speak.

Still, understanding that truth didn't come easy.

When I decided to start my transportation company in 2016, I had no substantial savings account and no mentor to show me the ropes. I had just a vision—and a whole lot of lessons waiting to unfold.

I remember signing my first contract with a company. The rep told me, "You're going to start within thirty days." I was excited, focused, and ready to go. I started preparing everything. But weeks passed. No updates. No calls. Just silence.

Eventually, I found out she no longer worked there. My contract had been sitting on someone's desk the entire time— never making it to corporate in Atlanta. All that time, I had been waiting for something that wasn't even in motion.

Then I was told something that rocked me: "The rules changed. You now need a wheelchair van to get started."

I was stunned.

I had already stretched myself financially just to get to this point. Now they were telling me I needed more—more money, more compliance, more time. For a second, I felt defeated. I questioned everything. Was this really for me? Had I missed the mark?

But then, I caught myself.

I remembered who I was. I remembered what I had written. I remembered that energy doesn't lie. If I wanted this, I couldn't afford to dwell in frustration. I had to shift my frequency. I had to refocus—not on what I lacked, but on what I wanted to create.

And once I did that, things moved fast.

Within a week, I found the perfect wheelchair-accessible van. It was like it was waiting for me to align my energy. Not because I had it all figured out, but because I finally chose faith over fear.

That was the start of my first business. Not just a company, but a calling.

Since then, I've learned that there will always be delays, detours, and discouragements. But none of that can stop a man who's tuned into the right frequency.

The biggest breakthrough came during one of the hardest seasons of my life. My son was battling depression and spiritual confusion. And as his father, I didn't know how to fix it. I was running my business on the outside, but on the inside, I was falling apart.

One day, I walked into my bathroom, turned on the faucet, and slid down the wall. I cried from a place I didn't know existed. I whispered, "God, why is this happening? Why now?"

And in that quiet moment, I heard something inside say: *You're still here because your story isn't over. But you have to shift.*

That voice reminded me that pain is not meant to punish—it's meant to position.

So I chose gratitude again.

Not for the circumstances, but for the strength I hadn't realized I had. For the vision that hadn't left me. For the future that was still calling me forward. I stopped vibrating at the level of fear and started aligning with peace—even in the middle of chaos.

And that shift? It changed everything.

I started noticing small miracles—divine alignments. The right people. Unexpected doors opening. Favor I couldn't explain. My clarity deepened. My rest improved. My conversations felt richer. I realized I had tapped into a new station.

It had always been there. I had just been tuned out.

And once I understood that, everything began to shift.

I started walking differently. Talking differently. I stopped trying to force things and started attracting them. I started pouring into others from overflow, not from depletion.

And this is where my life truly changed.

Not in the big wins, but in the daily choices to stay in alignment, to be honest with my energy, and to trust my inner guidance more than the noise around me.

I realized you don't attract what you want—you attract what you *are*.

And that means your internal world will always manifest externally—eventually.

The more I lived in that truth, the more I saw my life evolve. I began mentoring others—not just on logistics or business growth but on belief, energy, alignment, and showing up as the version of you that already has what you're praying for.

So, the things I've learned from my journey are these:

TIME DOESN'T BLOCK YOU—IT MIRRORS YOU

If you're aligned, things flow faster. If you're out of sync, they feel stuck. Time is just a mirror showing you the state of your energy.

ENERGY WILL NEVER LIE TO YOU

You can say all the right words, read all the right books—but if your spirit isn't congruent, your results won't be either.

GRATITUDE IS NOT OPTIONAL—IT'S FOUNDATIONAL

It's not something you wait to feel. It's something you choose. And when you choose it, you shift the room. You shift your results. You shift your reality.

So now, every single day, I give thanks. Not just for the good—but for the growth. For the moments that humbled me. For the ones that healed me. And for the ones that keep reminding me: You're not behind. You're just being aligned.

I speak to young men who feel like their value is invisible. I encourage women who feel like no one sees their struggle. I remind entrepreneurs that the business they're building is more than numbers—it's an energetic legacy.

When you raise your frequency, you raise your future. You don't have to chase it. You have to *choose* it.

And if there's one thing I know now, it's this: Once you've tasted alignment, you'll never settle for anything less. Because when you vibrate on purpose, you live on purpose. And life meets you at that level.

So, I'll ask you the same question I had to ask myself:

What would shift if you aligned your energy with your desires?

What could change if you showed up like your future was already calling you by name?

You don't need permission. You need alignment. And everything you're looking for is already looking for you.

You just have to match its signal.

CLEVELAND AUZENNE

Cleveland Auzenne is the proud owner of IRIDE Transportation, a company dedicated to providing safe and reliable non-emergency medical transportation services. As a Certified Instructor with the Napoleon Hill Foundation, he empowers others through the timeless principles of success, mindset, and purpose. Serving as Vice President of the Southwest Louisiana Black Chamber of Commerce, Cleveland is a passionate advocate for economic growth, small business support, and community advancement.

A devoted husband to his incredible wife and a loving father, Cleveland leads with integrity, faith, and a deep love for people. He is committed to uplifting those around him and helping individuals align with their highest potential—both personally and professionally. Whether mentoring entrepreneurs, volunteering locally, or speaking on the power of mindset and perseverance, Cleveland believes that service, gratitude, and love are the true currency of success. His mission is clear: to build, serve, and inspire from the inside out.

Author's Website: *www.IRidesTransportation.com*

Book Series Website: *www.TheBookOfFrequency.com*

DR. CURT COLLINS

FAITH, FREQUENCY, & THE FREEDOM TO RISE

"In all circumstances give thanks; for this is the will of God in Christ Jesus for you."
~ **Thessalonians 5:18**

In life, we don't always get to choose what happens. Challenges arise without warning. Pain arrives uninvited. Uncertainty, heartbreak, betrayal, and loss weave themselves into the very fabric of our lives. Yet alongside them exist joy, deep human connection, and moments of pure bliss. Life is paradoxical and unfolds without our consent. What we can choose, however, is how we respond, and that choice is everything.

For me, learning to become aware of my emotional frequency and then practicing intentionality has been an amazing gift that has served me well. I learned to raise my emotional frequency from lower vibrational states of guilt, fear, and anger into higher ones like courage, love, and gratitude. The faster you can identify the emotion that is not serving your higher self, breathe it in, and feel it intensely enough to release it back into the ether from which it came, the faster you will begin to write the future tales in your book of life. When you begin to use your emotions consistently to fuel the greatest version of yourself, the universe and all its resources start to align with you.

Once you live fully at cause rather than effect to your outer happenings, your dreams seem to come true at a much faster rate. Love and gratitude are not simply emotional reactions to good circumstances; they are transformational forces that can transmute pain into growth, hardship into healing, and adversity into victory.

As a chiropractor working with patients for over two decades, I have seen firsthand the cost of living at lower frequencies. People trapped in chronic blame, who are angry at others, at themselves, at God, inevitably end up manifesting emotional and physical symptoms: Persistent fatigue, chronic pain, mysterious illnesses without clear diagnoses, and treatments that never fully resolve their complaints. We are, in essence, energetic beings expressing ourselves through physical form.
What we carry within, we magnify and project outward. And the world responds accordingly.

When we vibrate at the level of peace, compassion, and gratitude, life reflects that same energy back to us. The difference between living the life of our dreams and enduring a nightmare we can't wake up from often comes down to the vibrational frequency we hold onto most consistently.

Many don't realize that emotions are not just passing mental events. They are energetic frequencies. The more emotionally charged the event, the stronger the imprint it leaves on the subconscious mind. As children, we are unable to filter what we absorb. We take everything in. The positive and negative alike. Our minds are like unprotected computers accepting unfiltered programming. This is why childhood trauma is so damaging and why it becomes the invisible force behind so much suffering later in life.

Yet as adults, we are given the incredible gift of choice. No one can make us hold onto negative events once they have fully lived out their purpose without our permission. Herein lies our greatest power, the ability to attune our consciousness to higher frequencies and consciously shape our destiny in the direction of our choice.

Through his books *Power vs. Force* and *Letting Go,* Dr. David Hawkins profoundly impacted my understanding of this truth. In *Letting Go,* he laid out emotional frequencies and numbered the tone levels from 20 to 1,000 on a logarithmic scale, creating what he called the Map of Consciousness. His work shifted the way I view the world and changed how I respond to life's inevitable challenges.

Hawkins' research revealed that the lowest frequencies, such as shame (20), guilt (3), and apathy (5), are heavy contractive states where hope seems absent and life feels impossible. Just getting out of bed can be challenging for those stuck in these states. Fear (100), anger (150), and pride (175) may be more active, but they still operate from ego, separation, and resistance. Although these emotions can initially fuel action to escape from despair, if we stay locked in them, they ultimately prolong suffering. Not because life is intended to be cruel, but because we are tuned into a signal that receives what we project.

At the vibrational level of 200, the scale tips toward empowerment. Courage (200) and acceptance (350) begin to break down the walls of the ego and allow God's grace to flow. It is at the frequency of love (500) that a profound shift occurs. Here, life is no longer something to endure, but rather something to trust as we learn to let go of our instinct to control it. Gratitude, a close companion to love, amplifies this frequency, creating a magnetic field of healing, synchronicity, and clarity. This is the energetic space where our intentionality turns into miracles.

Dr. Hawkins' research showed that a single individual living consistently at the frequency of love has the energetic capacity to counterbalance the negativity of 750,000 people operating below the level of 200. One individual vibrating at enlightenment can literally elevate the consciousness of the entire planet. History's greatest spiritual teachers have embodied this reality. It is humbling and empowering to realize that the simple daily choice to live in love, to forgive, to express gratitude regardless of outer circumstances, can literally help uplift the entire world.

Life has certainly tested me with plenty of challenges. I watched my mother battle cancer and pass away during the summer after my freshman year of college. I went through a painful divorce and custody battle that resulted in being alienated indefinitely from my twelve-year-old daughter. I aligned with the wrong business partners and battled insurance companies that refused to pay hundreds of thousands of dollars owed to our practice.

Eventually, this all snowballed together and proved to be more than I could manage, leading to overwhelming debt and bankruptcy. Just as I began to rebuild, a new test arrived. After recommending a patient explore stem cell therapy instead of risky surgery or addictive medications, the chiropractic board attempted to strip away my license and my life's work.

I will never forget standing in my office, celebrating new milestones, feeling back in the driver's seat of my destiny, when I was served the complaint. As I read through the allegations, something surprising stirred within me. I felt joy begin to bubble up. At that moment, I knew I would not just survive this attack, but I would use it as fuel to rise even higher. I would not let fear or injustice dictate my future. I would double down on my mission to help people have access to all healing options.

I have seen too many people in similar situations surrender to bitterness and resentment. The pain and disappointment became more than they could endure, and they took the path that ultimately led to a life of regret, disappointment, and unfulfilled dreams. I chose a different path. Armed with the knowledge that my emotional frequency determines my destiny, I chose to release anger in that moment and replace it with love and gratitude.

One of the greatest blessings that emerged during these difficult years was meeting the amazing woman who would become my wife—a partner whose unwavering love, support, and encouragement proved stronger than any self-doubt or opposition I faced. Together, we have built a life filled with joy, gratitude, growth, and deep trust in the path God has laid before us. I truly believe that had I succumbed to the lesser emotions of anger and resentment, I would have missed the opportunity to meet the woman of my dreams, and the life we have created together would have been lost to me.

The greatest power we possess is not in changing our circumstances but in choosing the frequency from which we meet them. Love and gratitude are not emotional byproducts; they are advanced spiritual technologies. When you align with them, you elevate not only your own life but the energetic field of everyone you encounter. Healing begins. Guidance appears. Peace prevails. This is the true path to freedom. This is how you rise from the ashes and build something extraordinary— something worthy of the gift of life you have been entrusted with.

The frequency you choose today shapes the reality you live tomorrow—so choose love, choose gratitude, and watch the miracles unfold.

CURT COLLINS

Dr. Curt Collins is a visionary chiropractor, regenerative medicine expert, and founder of Tomorrow Doctor. Since 2001, he has specialized in upper cervical chiropractic care and integrative wellness, blending time-tested principles with new innovative therapies. As Clinic Director at Envista Medical Neck & Back Center in Bakersfield, CA, he leads a multidisciplinary team dedicated to restoring health and relieving pain through advanced treatments, including stem cell and regenerative medicine.

Dr. Collins also co-founded Level 3 Consulting, where he mentors doctors nationwide to scale practices, automate operations, and create lasting impact without burnout. Grounded in faith and driven by purpose, he believes health is our greatest wealth, our networks determine our net worth, and service is life's highest calling. Whether in practice, on stage, or guiding groups, his mission is to awaken human potential, elevate frequency, and inspire others to live a higher quality life filled with health, happiness, and success.

Author's Website: *www.TomorrowDoctor.com*

Book Series Website: *www.TheBookOfFrequency.com*

CYNTHIA DEL ROSARIO

TUNING IN: LOVE & SELF-AWARENESS CHANGE LIVES

When I think about frequency, I think of energy, not just the energy around us, but the energy within. It's a subtle current flowing from a person, place, or group, a vibration you don't see but feel deep in your body, like a quiet hum just beneath the surface of awareness. Every day, I learn more about the energy I exude, how I'm perceived, and how others receive me.

Equally important is my ability to tune into the energy around me. The moment I step into a room, I ask, "What's the energy here? Are we clashing, or are we aligned? Because ultimately, this awareness shapes how we connect, grow, and move with intention.

People often enter spaces without tuning into the frequency, and as a result, they miss the mark. They don't realize they're either harmonizing with the room's energy or creating dissonance within it. Over time, I've learned that some people carry a clear sense of purpose, what I call "Mission Energy." Others show up with generosity and warmth, the "Giver Energy." And then there are those who bring chaos or tension wherever they go. In those moments, it's best to step back and protect your own energy. But every so often, everything clicks, everyone is aligned, and those are the moments that truly shine.

Every day is a new chance to check your frequency. What's your intention? Who do you surround yourself with? Who's in your sandbox? What energy will you allow in or let go of today? The frequency you hold becomes the path you walk.

FREQUENCY IS VISIBLE—IF YOU LOOK FOR IT

Although frequency is invisible to the eye, it's incredibly visible in how people move, interact, and exist. You can see intentions. You can feel them. Why are you here? Why are you continuing that relationship, that job, that conversation—even when it no longer serves you?

I've learned to really observe people, to see them for who they are beneath the surface. I often find myself saying, "I see you." I see your intentions, your energy, and your patterns. When I meet people for the first time in group settings, I prefer to sit back, not be invisible, but take it all in. I observe with the intention of understanding the frequency and flow. How do others interact with them? What kind of presence do they carry? That tells you so much.

Tuning into the frequencies around you can transform the way you move through both your personal and professional life.

Take my daughter and husband, for example—they share similar frequencies, and over time, I've learned to recognize when they're open and when they're not. If the vibe is off, I don't force the conversation. Sometimes, just being there and letting them share their day means more than anything. Knowing how to show up in the right way, at the right time, is essential for staying aligned. When their energy is grounded and clear, I know I can expect more because their energy matches their potential.

LOVE WITHOUT STRINGS

People think love has to come with rules. You have to talk every day, show up to everything, or be in constant contact. That's not how I love. I have friends, men and women, who know that if they call me and say, "I need your help," I'm there. No questions asked. That's real love.

There's a powerful story by Simon Sinek where he shares that sometimes you just need eight minutes to change someone's day. Just eight minutes to vent, cry, scream, or say what needs to be said, enough to create a deep emotional impact. Now, I tell my friends, "If you're feeling low or need support, just ask me if I have eight minutes. I'll stop what I'm doing, and I'll give you those eight minutes because I know it's serious." We are all busy. We have careers, kids, obligations, lives that pull us in all directions. But we can give eight minutes—and in those eight minutes, we give love.

On the flip side, there are people I love, but I'll never spend time with them. That's real love, too. I'll love you from afar, because your frequency doesn't align with mine. I don't want to spend my day soaking in complaints or negativity. That's not selfish—it's self-care.

And that's the truth about love. It doesn't always require a conversation, a gift, or an ongoing relationship. Sometimes love just means you're there when it counts.

GROWING UP IN THE CHAOS OF FREQUENCY

I am a fighter. Always have been. I'm the youngest of six, born to a father who had children with four different women. From an early age, I had to find ways to stand out. As the baby, I was spoiled, and I didn't realize some of my siblings resented me for it. Looking back, I feel bad about what I did to my brother. I used to point fingers and blame him for everything. He always took the fall. I didn't understand the weight of those actions or the long-term impact.

I didn't understand energy then, or how resentment shaped a room. But I was in it, and that pattern followed me into adulthood.

Throughout my career, I often found myself recruited by executives who knew me personally. "Come work for me," they'd say. "We need someone like you." But to others, I was just seen as "the boss's friend." Maybe they felt I didn't deserve it, maybe they assumed I got special treatment, but I didn't. I worked harder than anyone else in the room just to prove I belonged. I didn't want a handout. I wanted a seat at the table. I've always been a fighter, and I earned my place.

Still, the energy around me whispered otherwise. And I had to fight through that, too.

LESSONS FROM MY PARENTS' FREQUENCIES

My parents ran a dry-cleaning business together, and I saw firsthand how different frequencies can create conflict, even when the goal is the same.

My mom could work in chaos. She knew where every piece of clothing was—even if they weren't organized. My dad, on the other hand, needed everything in order. Twos with twos. Threes with threes. If it wasn't organized, it wasn't right to him.

They often argued over how things should be done. But here's what I learned from that: You can work in completely different ways, and still move toward the same goal. And if you don't take time to see that—to really see it—you miss the big picture. They weren't listening to each other. They were so focused on the process that they lost sight of the outcome. And because of that, they missed the love. They missed the alignment.

That stayed with me. It taught me that frequency isn't just about harmony—it's about purpose. It's about being able to say, "We're different, but we're working toward the same goal."

PIVOTING IN LOVE & LEADERSHIP

One of the most powerful lessons I've learned recently is about my own patterns. I've always been the person who pushes forward, who leads the charge, who sees the goal and goes for it. But I never paused to ask myself: "What are my patterns?"

A mentor once taught me, "The way you do one thing is the way you do everything." And that hit hard. I started to see it.

Every time I wasn't supported, I'd leave. I'd say, "We're no longer aligned," and I'd walk away. That was my default pivot.

But now, I've learned that sometimes the pivot isn't an exit. Sometimes, it's a deeper question. "Is this truly misalignment, or is this an opportunity to grow?" As the CEO, I can't just walk away anymore. I have to assess, realign, and re-commit when it's right.

And through that, I've realized something else: You've got to look outside your usual circles. When you're stuck, it's probably because you're tapping into the same frequency pool. Maybe the solution isn't in the room—it's in the next room. Or the next industry. Or the next relationship.

PATTERNS, PURPOSE, & THE POWER OF SELF-REFLECTION

If you want to grow, ask yourself: What have I done consistently? What patterns do I repeat in work, in love, in life?

For me, I always left. That was my pattern. I knew who I was. I was confident. But sometimes, confidence without reflection leads to stagnation. I had to start asking harder questions, and those questions led me to examine how everything is interconnected.

Because here's the truth: You are one whole person. You can't separate who you are at home from who you are in business. If your kid gets sick, your business gets affected. If your team is toxic, you bring that energy home. You are one. And the frequency or energy you hold in one part of your life shows up in the other, whether you want it to or not.

Dr. Masaru Emoto's research showed that positive and negative energy can shape the molecular structure of water. He found that water exposed to kind words and loving intentions formed beautiful, harmonious ice crystals, while negative words and feelings produced distorted, unpleasant patterns. Since our bodies are mostly water, this study highlights how our thoughts, emotions, and daily frequency deeply influence not only ourselves but also the world around us.

So ask yourself: What's the pattern of your energy? Are you surrounded by loving, positive people? Or do toxic vibes persist day after day?

LOVE IS A DAILY COMMITMENT

I like to think of love the way I think of water hitting stone. You can throw a whole bucket of water at a rock, and it won't change a thing. But drop by drop, day by day, the stone gives way. Not because the water is stronger, but because it's consistent.

That's how love works. That's how leadership works. That's how relationships work. Show up
every day. Be consistent. Love even when it's inconvenient. Lead even when it's hard. Speak even when no one is listening.

You can't say, "I love you" one day and then treat someone terribly the next. You can't build trust in a moment. It takes time. It takes proof. Over and over again.

The energy you radiate shapes every aspect of your life, including your relationships, leadership, and personal growth. When you consistently tune in, reflect on your patterns, and consciously choose who and what you welcome into your space, you unlock the power to intentionally shape your journey.

This is more than a habit—it's a powerful discipline. The discipline of frequency.

CYNTHIA DEL ROSARIO

Cynthia Del Rosario is a visionary leader whose steadfast integrity and inspiring spirit fuel her dedication to serving communities and developing innovative solutions with lasting impact. With over forty years of industry experience, Cynthia's career spans a broad spectrum of content creation, marketing, production, distribution, talent and rights management, and business affairs. She has collaborated with some of the world's leading brands, including Verizon, GE Capital, Procter & Gamble, Pfizer, IBM, Pepsi, and American Express.

As founder of 7 Mile Global Ad Solutions, LLC, she leads efforts to transform how branded intellectual property is managed, creating platforms such as IP360 and the 7MG Academy. Alongside her husband, Patrick Neville—an Iraq War veteran and 9/11 First Responder—she owns a popular bar and restaurant, Whiskey River NY, that fosters connection, community, and memorable conversation.

Her proudest achievements are her two children, Kayla and Aidan.

Author's Website: *www.7MilesGlobal.com*

Book Series Website: *www.TheBookOfFrequency.com*

DANIEL KILBURN

THE FREQUENCY WE LIVE ON

Well, hello again. If you've found your way to this chapter, chances are we've already shared some space—either in person, in print, or in spirit. And if we haven't yet, let's just pretend we're sitting together across a warm cup of coffee, talking about something that matters.

Love and gratitude. Those words carry more weight than most people are prepared to hold. And the truth is, I didn't always know what they really meant—at least not the way I understand them now. That's what this chapter is about. Not an instruction manual, not a grand sermon—just one man's walk through the fog of life, fumbling toward clarity, and finding, time and again, that the light at the end of the tunnel was love. And the ground beneath that light was gratitude.

When I started thinking about what I wanted to contribute to this book, I found myself in a familiar place—talking out loud to myself, pacing the floor, asking the universe what I had to say that might mean something to someone else. And it hit me. I wasn't writing this just for the reader. I was writing it for me, too. Maybe mostly for me. Not out of ego, but out of necessity.

Because writing has always helped me make sense of the things I can't say out loud. It's the mirror I hold up when I need to check my own pulse.

There's this idea I've held onto for a long time, that each of us is here for a reason. Now, we might not know that reason right away—or even ever—but it's there, quietly calling us to rise. And no, I don't think that reason is just to collect things or climb ladders. I don't believe we're here just to accumulate stuff, fill closets, or chase fleeting pleasures. I believe we're here to learn something—and maybe more importantly, to teach something. To become something and then turn around and help someone else become, too.

That brings me back to love. Not the romantic kind, though that has its place. I'm talking about the kind of love that sees beyond skin and circumstance. The kind of love that begins with self-awareness and ends with service. The kind that says, "I'm here, I matter, and so do you."

Now, I'll be honest with you: I haven't always loved myself. In fact, there were times when I didn't even like myself. I'd look in the mirror and see a man weighed down by doubt, by choices that didn't serve me, by guilt I hadn't processed. And in those moments, loving others felt like a performance—an act I put on rather than a truth I lived. How could I truly love others if I couldn't love myself? That question sat with me like a stone in my pocket. Heavy. Always there.

But little by little, I started to realize that loving yourself isn't vanity—it's responsibility. It's not about thinking you're perfect or putting yourself above others. It's about recognizing your own worth so you can reflect that worth back to the world. Like shining a flashlight into a dark room, self-love lights the path not just for you, but for anyone else walking beside you.

And as that love for self began to grow, so did something else —gratitude. A quiet, persistent kind of gratitude that crept in during the in-between moments. The early morning silence. The hum of tires on asphalt. The second breath after a deep sigh. I found myself being grateful just to be above ground, grateful to have another day to try again. There's an old saying, "Every day above ground is a good day." Turns out, that's not just a bumper sticker. It's a survival mantra.

But gratitude isn't always loud. It doesn't always come wrapped in fireworks or fanfare. Sometimes it's found in simple acts, like holding a door open, smiling at a stranger, or picking up a piece of trash someone else walked past. These aren't heroic gestures. They won't make headlines. But they're seeds, and every seed sown in kindness has the potential to grow roots in someone else's heart.

I was raised to be courteous. Open doors, say please and thank you, and help those who need it. And I've tried to carry that forward in my life, not because it makes me feel noble, but because it makes me feel human. And maybe, just maybe, if someone sees me doing a small thing—like tossing a missed piece of trash into the bin—they'll do the same. Not out of obligation, but out of a shared sense of ownership, community, and of gratitude.

That brings me to something I learned the hard way: the importance of receiving. See, for most of my life, I had this knee-jerk reaction whenever someone offered to help me. I'd wave it off, say "I've got it," even when I clearly didn't. I thought I was being strong and self-sufficient. But the truth? I was being closed off. I was rejecting not just their kindness, but their need to give it. Because here's what I've come to understand—receiving is not weakness. It's grace.

There are people in this world who find joy in helping others, just like I do. And when we block their generosity, we're not protecting ourselves—we're robbing them of the chance to give. Accepting a gift, an act of kindness, a hand on your shoulder—it's not a burden. It's an act of courage. It's saying, "Yes, I see you. I trust you. I believe I'm worthy."

That shift changed me. I started saying yes more often—not just to help, but to healing. Not just to support, but to connect. And the more I said yes, the more I felt plugged into something bigger than myself.

And here's the beautiful part: Once you start living from that place of self-love and gratitude, you start walking with purpose. You begin to understand that every decision you make sends out a frequency—a vibration that affects not just your own life, but the lives around you.

I gave a speech recently at a Toastmasters contest called "The Power of a Single Decision." Truly, every shift begins with one choice—one yes, one no, one pause. Even choosing to do nothing is still a choice. And each choice either tunes us closer to our highest selves or pulls us off-key.

This idea of frequency—it's not just poetic. It's practical. Think of it like tuning a radio. If your signal is love and gratitude, then you're going to attract conversations, opportunities, and people that resonate with that same energy. But if you're stuck in bitterness, resentment, or fear, your frequency will pull you into places that reinforce that dissonance.

So, I try to tune myself daily. Some days, I'm a little off. That's okay. But every night before I sleep, I ask myself a simple question: Did I help someone today? If the answer is yes, I sleep better. If it's no, I think about how I can do better tomorrow. And then I do.

This chapter is more than words on a page. It's a reflection of how I've learned to walk through this life. I've stumbled. I've fallen. But I've also risen, again and again, on the wings of love and gratitude. And I believe—truly—that if more of us tuned into those frequencies, the world wouldn't just be a better place. It would be a more beautiful one.

So, as you turn the page, I leave you with this: love yourself first. Not because it's trendy, but because it's transformational. Practice gratitude—not as a habit, but as a way of seeing the world. Say yes to the people who show up for you and say yes to showing up for them. And above all, keep asking that question: Did I help someone today? Then let your answer guide the music of your life.

Because when all is said and done, it's not just about the legacy we leave behind. It's about the frequency we live on.

DANIEL KILBURN

Kilburn is a retired U.S. Army Senior Infantry Drill Sergeant, a seasoned speaker, and the founder of Emergency Action Planning LLC. With a heart for service and a mission to safeguard families and communities, Daniel dedicates his life to teaching the principles of resilience, preparedness, and financial literacy. His powerful voice and grounded wisdom stem not just from years of military discipline but from real-life experiences navigating natural disasters, personal challenges, and transformational growth. Daniel's work centers on helping people rediscover their sense of purpose and security, especially during life's most uncertain moments.

An award-winning Toastmaster and bestselling co-author, Daniel brings authenticity, clarity, and compassion to every page he writes. Through his words, he challenges readers to reflect, rise, and resonate on higher frequencies—starting with love and gratitude. For additional information, Daniel's contact information can be found here: www.linkedin.com/in/DanielKilburn

Author's Website: *www.EmergencyActionPlanning.com*

Book Series Website: *www.TheBookOfFrequency.com*

DANIELE G. LATTANZI

FROM UNLUCKY LOSER TO GRATEFUL WINNER

....

"Learn to be thankful for what you already have while you pursue all that you want."
~ Jim Rohn

A CURIOUS DISCOVERY

While reviewing the 2024 World Happiness Report, I observed an unexpected trend: a decline in happiness among individuals aged fifteen to twenty-four in North America and Western Europe since 2010. This statistic captured my interest. What accounts for this notable decrease? Could it be attributed to external pressures and cultural expectations, or perhaps the challenging phases of adolescence and youth itself? This finding led me to reflect on my own experiences, particularly when I was of a similar age in Italy.

"FEELING UNLUCKY:"
TRAPPED BY MY OWN PERCEPTION

As a teenager in Italy, I genuinely believed I was cursed—chronically unlucky. We even had a slang term for it: "sfigato," loosely translating to someone awkward, uncool, or simply not good enough at navigating life. That was precisely how I felt.

I distinctly remember wanting a specific Vespa scooter, an iconic Italian symbol of freedom and status, in my teenage years. It wasn't just a vehicle; it represented belonging, acceptance, and social standing. While all my friends had one, I was stuck with a fifteen-year-old moped—"not cool" in my perception.

Similarly, I had an enormous crush on a girl in my neighborhood. She was effortlessly cool, beautiful, and popular. Yet, I felt painfully inadequate—believing I lacked the necessary coolness or confidence to express my feelings. Mentally, I had conceded defeat before any attempt was made. Again, the recurring sentiment further reinforced my belief: "I'm just unlucky."

Another vivid example of my perceived misfortune revolved around school. Even though I generally received good grades, I struggled deeply with memory retention. I would study diligently, pass exams successfully, and achieve commendable results, only to find that mere months later, the material I had mastered seemed to vanish entirely from my mind—as if it had never been there. It was like staring at a blank page.

Looking around at my friends, I didn't notice this issue affecting them the same way, which naturally led me to wonder, *"Why me? Could I have early dementia? Was there something neurologically wrong with me?"* But was I truly unlucky, or was my perception more of an impediment than the actual reality?

LIVING ON GROUNDHOG DAY?

Looking back, another key aspect of that period was a feeling of missing opportunities and a sense of stagnant routine. Like the movie *Groundhog Day*, my days blended into a never-ending cycle of sameness.

At that time, there was no internet or social media; information came solely from traditional media and magazines. I was an avid reader of all types—culture, lifestyle, sports, and business. I had the impression that opportunities abounded, but they were all out of my reach. I felt trapped in an endless loop, unable to see any difference or progress from one week to the next. The feeling of being unlucky resurfaced. It became clear: I had to make a change to break this loop and shift my current scene.

I didn't recognize it at the time, but that was my first significant mindset shift. I asked myself, *"What can I do to change my situation? Something I control?"* The answer was clear: learning another language and advancing my education. This would improve my skill set and eventually open doors to new opportunities. That decision led me to apply for an international student exchange program, which resulted in a scholarship to study abroad in São Paulo, Brazil, marking the beginning of a transformative chapter.

THE VALUE OF EXTERNAL PERSPECTIVE

Moving from my small Italian hometown (population 40,000) to the sprawling metropolis of São Paulo, Brazil (13.5 million) was a profound culture shock. The new environment, the unfamiliar routine, and the fresh challenges pushed my sense of being "unlucky" into the background. It didn't disappear instantly, but the intensity of my surroundings diminished its hold.

As part of the exchange program, we were encouraged to immerse ourselves in the local culture. About four months into my Brazilian experience, our group visited a São Paulo favela. These impoverished neighborhoods, characterized by poor infrastructure, starkly contrasted with anything I knew.

There, I met several families, but one left an enduring impression. A family with two young children, an eleven-year-old girl and her younger brother (around eight or nine), radiated pure joy despite their challenging living conditions. I vividly recall watching them play soccer barefoot on a dusty dirt field with an old, worn ball. Their lack of proper gear, even shoes, didn't diminish their genuine enthusiasm. They laughed, shouted, and were utterly absorbed in the moment. Their eyes sparkled with hope, and their smiles were infectious.

Witnessing this scene struck a powerful chord within me, shattering my narrative of being unlucky. The stark contrast between my perceptions and their simple, authentic joy was undeniable. In that instant, the reasons behind my own feelings of misfortune seemed trivial. I recalled the Vespa I didn't get, the crush I never confessed to, and my concerns about memory. My focus on what I lacked changed significantly.

In its place emerged a profound sense of gratitude. For the first time, I understood that my earlier unhappiness stemmed from focusing solely on what I didn't have and viewing my circumstances from a skewed perspective. I had overlooked the countless blessings already present.

It became distinctly clear that I was far from unlucky; gratitude had simply found me. I felt immense appreciation for my supportive family in Italy and my generous host family in Brazil, who had welcomed me without obligation. My worries about learning were replaced by gratitude for this very experience, which pushed me to master a new language and recognize my own strength and resilience. I appreciated being one of only a hundred students selected for the scholarship.

Reflecting on this, I saw my capabilities in a new, empowering light. Since then, I've learned to view situations positively, acknowledge progress, appreciate those around me, and seek the good in every circumstance. This has paved the way for me to succeed and have a life filled with accomplishments, and, most importantly, the gratitude to help others.

ARE YOU INSIDE A JAR?

Blair Enns popularized the metaphor, "You can't read the label from inside the jar."

In conclusion, my student exchange experience offers these key takeaways:

* Being deeply immersed in your own situation—inside your "jar"—makes gaining the perspective needed for change difficult. While a move abroad isn't necessary, actively seek fresh perspectives to unlock new possibilities.

* Recognize your inherent power. Acknowledge your strengths, talents, and progress, regardless of external opinions.

* Stay positive. Gratitude fuels success by helping you identify solutions and opportunities you might otherwise miss.

Opportunities are all around you! Get out there and get them!

DANIELE G. LATTANZI

Daniele G. Lattanzi is your Practice Growth Partner with over twenty-five years of experience helping small businesses and healthcare practitioners transform their activity into thriving, scalable companies. His entrepreneurial journey builds on extensive management, finance, marketing, e-commerce, and business development expertise. Fluent in four languages—English, Italian, Portuguese, and Spanish—Daniele's linguistic skills have been instrumental in his international coaching and business operations across Italy, Europe, and North and South America.

As the Co-Founder and CEO of Effective Practice Management and Holistic Health Solutions since 2016, Daniele has dedicated himself to empowering private practice owners and their teams to unlock their full potential by providing proven practice management training and coaching. Follow him at: *www.Instagram.com/DG_Lattanzi*

Author's Website: *www.EffectivePracticeManagement.com*

Book Series Website: *www.TheBookOfFrequency.com*

DAWNESE OPENSHAW

WHISPERS OF GRACE: A HEART'S JOURNEY TO TRANSFORMATION

"Love is the highest frequency you can emit. The higher the frequency, the closer you are to the truth, to your power, and to the source."
~ **Rhonda Byrne**

No matter how often I'd heard that love and gratitude are two of the most powerful feelings, it wasn't until I found myself almost completely void of them that I finally had my own awareness—a personal awakening, we could call it.

I remember when love (and gratitude) felt like luxuries—beautiful, poetic ideas that belonged on inspirational wall art, but not inside the reality I was navigating called my life. I was deep in an endless cycle of letting life just happen to me, and I found myself pushing and performing to prove my worth and value. My energy was scattered, my body exhausted, and my relationships strained. I lived in a frequency of scarcity—of time, self-worth, and emotional bandwidth.

It wasn't until a moment of absolute surrender that things began to shift. I remember it clearly: I was standing in my kitchen, dishes piled high, my phone buzzing, and my teenage daughter yelling at me about something, and I felt myself spiraling. Something in me cracked wide open—not out of weakness, but rather out of a fierce desire for something different. I looked at my husband and said, "Something's gotta change."

That day, I began searching for something, anything, that would support me in creating the much-needed change I felt was imperative for me to find joy. I remembered hearing how powerful practicing gratitude could be and thought, "Oh, what the heck. I've got nothing to lose. Why not give it a try?"

So, I began an experiment—it needed to be a simple thing I knew I could start with and stick with over time, because the last thing I needed was something more to add to my overabundant to-do list. I started placing my hand on my heart every morning and saying, "Thank you. I'm listening," then I took a deep breath and opened my heart to feeling whatever emotion came up.

What happened was an absolute gift to myself (and my family). It was the feeling of grace—an understanding and compassion within myself and where I was in that moment, becoming present to only that moment in time and space.

This simple act changed everything for me. My very being felt deeply connected, rooted, and lighter all at the same time. In these moments, I felt the power of *being* grateful and letting love and grace fill my heart before setting out on my daily activities. It made a world of difference in how I approached everything and everyone throughout my day. It changed *me*.

LOVE & GRATITUDE ARE FREQUENCIES OF ENERGY POWERFUL ENOUGH TO SHIFT OUR PHYSIOLOGY

Most people think of love and gratitude as emotional responses. But they are also frequencies—measurable states of energy that shift our entire being. According to the HeartMath Institute, when we focus on appreciation or care, our actual heart rhythm creates coherence. This harmony between our heart and brain improves mental clarity, emotional stability, and even immune function. Harmony is where it's at! When I find myself in the space of alignment with my body, mind, heart, and spirit...this is where the magic happens. This is where I feel led by love and in my vision for my life.

The frequency of love restores and repairs. It is the vibration that heals hearts, shifts energy, and brings life into harmony. Love resonates at 528 Hz—a frequency long associated with healing, transformation, and DNA repair. Gratitude, when practiced intentionally, expands the heart field, amplifying our capacity for joy and connection.

LOVE & GRATITUDE CAN SHIFT OUR PERCEPTION & REALITY

As humans, we are energetic beings. The frequencies we hold shape everything—from our emotional states to our external experiences. When we live on a higher frequency:

- Our emotions become more balanced.
- Our thought patterns shift from fear to possibility.
- Our attraction and manifestation abilities amplify.

Love is magnetic. Gratitude is expansive. Together, they reprogram our frequency field and shift what we attract, who we attract, how we respond to, and move through the world. They can help us move from reactive patterns to creating how we live with intention.

"Gratitude unlocks the fullness of life.
It turns what we have into enough, and more."
~ Melody Beattie

Before I tuned into love and gratitude, my internal dialogue was dominated by lack: "I don't have enough time. I'm not doing enough. I'm not enough." I would wake up already anxious, scroll through my phone for validation, and feel disconnected from the very life I had built.

After I committed to anchoring into love and gratitude, the flow of my days changed. I began waking up and whispering, "Thank you for my life." I noticed beauty in ordinary moments

—a smile from a passerby, the warmth of sunlight through the window, the way my body moved as I walked. Gratitude made me fully available for love, giving it and receiving it. I became alive again.

THE NEUROSCIENCE OF LOVE & GRATITUDE

Let me geek out on you for a moment and share how science confirms what the heart already knows:

• Gratitude activates the brain's reward system, releasing dopamine and serotonin—chemicals that elevate mood, reduce anxiety, and foster resilience.

• Love, especially unconditional love, stimulates the release of oxytocin, the bonding hormone. It deepens empathy, builds trust, and helps us feel safe in connection.

• Both love and gratitude activate the prefrontal cortex—the part of the brain responsible for self-awareness, decision-making, and emotional regulation. When this part of the brain is active, we become more intentional, more compassionate, and more aligned.

When we choose love and gratitude, we're not just being spiritual—we're becoming more neurologically integrated, emotionally grounded, and energetically elevated. Below you will find a couple of tools to support your awakening to the power of gratitude and love—your journey to grace.

A DAILY PRACTICE: THE HEART COHERENCE RITUAL

You don't need an hour of meditation or a silent retreat in Bali to raise your frequency. Here's a simple daily practice you can try:

1. **Pause and Breathe**: Sit quietly for two to three minutes. Place your hand on your heart.

2. **Heart Focus**: Breathe slowly and deeply into your heart space.

3. **Heart Feeling**: Recall a moment you felt deep love or gratitude. Let the feeling expand.

4. **Anchor and Repeat**: Whisper, "Thank you," as you breathe. Let that energy guide your next action.

This practice recalibrates your nervous system and raises your emotional baseline. Over time, you'll begin to default to love instead of fear, to gratitude instead of judgment.

A SEVEN-DAY RAISE YOUR FREQUENCY CHALLENGE

Shift your state, shift your frequency.

- For seven days, begin and end each day with a gratitude ritual.

- Each morning, write down three things you're grateful for and say them aloud.

- Each evening, reflect on one moment where you felt or expressed love.

- If you feel low or reactive during the day, pause, breathe into your heart, and whisper, "Thank you."

Watch what happens. You may notice that your conversations become softer, your intuition sharpens, and your energy expands.

Love and gratitude aren't passive.

Love and gratitude are intentional, conscious choices we make every moment, especially when life feels hard. They are also doorways that lead us back to ourselves, back to those we love, and back to a world where grace is always present.

You don't need to wait for something outside you to change. The frequency of love and gratitude is already within you, ready to tune you into the life you were meant to live.

Tune in. Say thank you. And let love lead.

DAWNESE OPENSHAW

Dawnese Openshaw is a visionary leader, master transformational and relationship coach, and passionate advocate for conscious living and loving. As Founder of Lead the Change, she empowers individuals, families, and organizations to lead with emotional, social, and relationship intelligence. Dawnese is the co-creator of the Global Leadership Experience, a life-changing training for those ready to align with their purpose and live a vision-led life.

A lifelong student of leadership since reading Dale Carnegie's *How to Win Friends and Influence People* at fourteen, Dawnese shares her experience and wisdom gained from daily living and supporting individual and organizational growth for over thirty years.

She and her husband, Scott, are celebrating thirty years of marriage, are proud parents of three amazing adult children, and are brand-new grandparents. Dawnese believes that when people live in alignment with their values, relationships thrive —and when relationships thrive, *magic happens.*

Author's Website: *www.LeadTheChange.org*

Book Series Website: *www.TheBookOfFrequency.com*

DHARMI SHAH

GRATITUDE, GROWTH, & A GLASS OF WINE

THE UNEXPECTED GIFT OF GRATITUDE

For as long as I can remember, I believed love was defined by one thing: being a mother. It was the picture-perfect idea of love, and for a long time, I couldn't see beyond it. I couldn't even begin to imagine that love could be something else, something different.

Then came loss. And more loss. Infertility, disappointment, and heartache began to chip away at the person I thought I was. The woman I envisioned myself to be—the one wrapped up in her identity as a wife and a mother—slowly started to slip away. I was left with a void that I wasn't sure how to fill. I had no idea who I was anymore. Who was I if I wasn't these things? Who was I if I wasn't in the roles that had been my idea of love all along?

It was one of the most painful, frustrating, and confusing times in my life. But, as they say, time has a way of healing, or at least reshaping the way we see things. Through heartache, self-reflection, and healing, I began to realize something unexpected—something I hadn't seen coming at all. I found love, but not in the way I had anticipated. Instead of chasing love, I began to discover a love that was already there. It was the love of gratitude.

THE TURNING POINT: FINDING LOVE IN MYSELF

This wasn't a dramatic "aha!" moment, but more like a gradual shift, a slow, almost imperceptible change in perspective. It was as though I had been looking through a foggy window for so long, straining to see what was outside, only to realize one day that the window had been open all along. I just hadn't noticed it. (And no, there were no twinkling fairy lights or dramatic music to accompany this realization. Although that would have been pretty cool.)

I started focusing on myself, but not in a self-centered way. I began to nurture my own well-being and happiness, a little like tending to a garden—slowly, carefully, and with patience. I didn't go searching for validation or love from others; instead, I began to realize that the love I needed the most was the love I had been neglecting to give myself.

I started embracing solitude, something I once feared. No longer did I see being alone as something to escape. Instead, I discovered the quiet peace that came with being content in my own company. I traveled more, built my career, and spent quality time with friends who had been sidelined while I had been too focused on an image of love that wasn't serving me.

JOY IN THE LITTLE THINGS (PIZZA INCLUDED)

And then there were the small moments—like the joy I felt eating an entire pizza by myself (with no shame, because, really, who's going to judge me?); the conversations with friends that made me laugh so hard I nearly snorted wine out of my nose; the late-night talks with people who truly understood me. Each of these moments added up, slowly but surely, helping me rebuild the person I had lost along the way.

Somewhere along this journey, something profound happened. I stopped seeing myself as broken, as someone who needed to be "fixed." I stopped waiting for life's betrayals to be righted. I stopped seeing love as something I had to fill a void with. Instead, I began to see love everywhere.

It was in the friendships that nurtured me, the family that supported me, and the simple yet profound acts of kindness that I encountered daily. I found love in quiet mornings with a cup of coffee, in the comfort of a late-night glass of wine that I could actually savor in peace. It wasn't about searching for something that was missing; it was about opening my eyes to the love that was already surrounding me.

THE GRATITUDE THAT CHANGED EVERYTHING

The real shift came when I began practicing gratitude—not as some fleeting, feel-good exercise, but as a true, deep appreciation for everything I had, for everything that was already present in my life. Instead of mourning the love I thought I had lost, I started appreciating the love I had all along. It was as if the lens through which I viewed my life had been polished, and suddenly everything appeared clearer, more vibrant. Kind of like cleaning your glasses after a week of wearing them with smudges and suddenly seeing the world in HD.

I became deeply grateful for my friends—those who showed up without asking for anything in return, those who listened, those who celebrated my successes, and stood by me in tough times. I realized that friends are often soulmates in disguise, and that love isn't confined to romantic relationships or parenthood.

I found myself feeling an immense sense of gratitude for my parents and family, for their unwavering support and love. I began to savor the moments we shared, from the simplest dinners to the more profound conversations that felt like lifelines.

FREEDOM TO CHOOSE MY OWN JOY

I started feeling grateful for the freedom I had to create my life, to make decisions that reflected my true self, to wake up each day knowing I was choosing my happiness. It was a radical shift in perspective. I was no longer tied to an idea of love that came with expectations or limitations. Instead, I was free to cultivate a life that resonated with me.

And, perhaps most importantly, I found gratitude for myself. The person I had become, the woman who had endured heartbreak, who had learned lessons, who had grown stronger and more compassionate. I had learned to love myself in a way I never had before, to treat myself with kindness and respect, and to recognize that I was already whole.

REDEFINING LOVE & HAPPINESS

Today, I no longer view love as something to be "found" or chased after. It's not a distant goal or some ideal I need to measure up to. Love is everywhere. It's in the connections we build, in the kindness we give and receive, and in the moments we share with others and ourselves. It's in the understanding that I am enough, that my worth is not defined by my marital status or whether I am a mother. I no longer feel the pressure to chase a certain version of love. Instead, I have learned to embrace the love that already surrounds me.

Happiness, too, is something I now see differently. It isn't tied to a particular outcome or milestone. It's in the life I've created, in the people I hold dear, and in the experiences that fill my soul with contentment. It's in the quiet confidence that comes with knowing that I am enough, just as I am.

LETTING GO OF THE CHASE

This journey has taught me that love isn't about possession, about clinging to an ideal or a dream. It's about embracing the love that is already present in your life. In that realization, I've found peace and joy that surpass anything I could have imagined before.

Love isn't just tied to the roles I once imagined for myself. It's in the laughter shared with friends, in the comfort of family, and in the quiet moments of self-acceptance. Love is in gratitude, and through gratitude, I've found everything I was looking for.

MY RECIPE FOR HAPPINESS

Here's the secret ingredient to my happiness:

- An abundance of belly laughs
- Boundless love
- An incredible amount of gratitude (because when life gives you lemons...)
- And just a dash of adventure to keep life spicy

It's simple, but it works. And it's the recipe I'll be following from here on out. Because, in the end, it's not about what we thought we were missing—it's about recognizing and savoring what we already have. And trust me, that's more than enough.

DHARMI SHAH

Dharmi Shah is a globally recognized, award-winning entrepreneur, celebrated for her transformative leadership and exceptional impact across industries. As the visionary founder of The Corporate Experience, a cutting-edge marketing firm, Dharmi curates unparalleled experiences that help businesses grow and thrive, all while forging lasting bonds that drive sustained success.

She is also the mastermind behind Refresh and Revitalize, an award-winning coaching brand dedicated to empowering women, cultivating a powerful community where they uplift, inspire, and support one another to reach their fullest potential.

Dharmi founded Evenings of Elegance, an elite event production company that spent over two decades creating extraordinary, high-profile events, leaving a lasting impression on every client. A culinary connoisseur, Dharmi finds pure joy in the kitchen, believing that the dinner table is where cherished memories, laughter, and joy come together, building profound connections with every shared meal.

Author's Website: *www.DharmiShah.com*

Book Series Website: *www.TheBookOfFrequency.com*

EILEEN E. GALBRAITH

TALES FROM BEYOND: LOVE FROM BEYOND THE GRAVE

Zeus made his grand exit from this earthly plane on April 10, 2022. But let's be real—he never really left. Every morning, I still say, "Good morning" to his picture like he's about to saunter in and demand fresh water from the faucet. Every night, I whisper, "Good night," fully expecting to hear a gentle *thump* on the end of the bed like he used to do, claiming his rightful throne.

His paw print is framed, his photos still on display, and his food bowl? Let's just say it took a while to retire it. Not because we were in denial (well, okay, maybe a little), but because love like his leaves behind paw prints that no vacuum could ever suck up.

Now Cleo—our elegant white short-haired with black tail queen—was adopted alongside Zeus. She always carried herself like feline royalty, and Zeus was her loyal jester. At first, I thought she was fine after his passing. Stoic. Unbothered. But then, the subtle signs began: She followed me room to room like my furry little life coach, curled up in my lap more frequently—finally enjoying some solo cuddle time without Zeus trying to photobomb her snuggles.

We kept Zeus's routines alive for a while, his bowl in place, his blanket folded just the way he liked it, his favorite spot by the window left untouched. I told myself it was for Cleo, but honestly? It was for me. His absence echoed in those small spaces. Even twenty-five weeks later, my heart would still skip a beat at the sound of a faint meow or the feeling of something brushing my leg (though sometimes it was just a rogue sock... but still).

Zeus was a once-in-a-lifetime cat. The kind of soul who didn't need much—just love, a sunbeam, and occasional bacon crumbs. He didn't eat human food, per se, but he had *opinions* about your snacks. Potato chips? He was there for the salt. Bacon? He'd magically appear before the pan even sizzled.

He was also a master trip artist. Walk too quickly without looking down, and you'd find yourself doing an impromptu interpretive dance in the kitchen. Zeus called it bonding. We called it hazardous.

And then there were the dreams.

About two months after he passed, I dreamt I walked into the kitchen and there he was—at his water bowl, cool as ever. He looked up at me, did his signature slow blink, and then wound around my legs like he never left. I knelt down, whispered, "Hi baby boy, what are you doing here?" and instantly felt the peace he came to deliver.

A few months later, I folded the throw blanket on the couch (his favorite snuggle spot), turned around for just a second, and boom, dream-Zeus was curled up on top of it, looking at me like, *"Took you long enough."* I turned to my husband and said, "Did you see him?" He didn't. But my heart did. And it smiled all night.

Zeus was our greeter, our comic relief, our cuddle monster. And then—on June 10, 2023—Cleo joined him in the stars. My heart shattered. She was my baby girl, my shadow, my silent comforter through the ache of missing Zeus. She was the grounding presence that reminded me to breathe.

And just like her brother, Cleo had her quirks. She was the queen of lap naps, purr therapy, and side-eye judgment. She had a way of silently staring into your soul like she knew all your secrets—and still loved you anyway. That's real love right there.

Losing them both has left a silence in my home that even the loudest TV can't drown out. But it's a silence filled with love. Because when a pet loves you, they don't just fill a house— they fill your heart. Forever.

You know, love shows up in many forms. We have the love of a partner, a parent, a sibling. And then... there's the pure, unconditional love of a pet. Zeus and Cleo didn't just coexist with us. They *loved* us. Every headbutt, every nap on our chests, every meow demanding attention—those were all tiny, furry, "I love yous."

Let me say this, too—I've been deeply blessed with the love of my husband, John. We've shared twenty beautiful years together, and I thank the Universe every day for bringing him into my life. Now, was he a cat guy? Not at first. But love makes us do wild things. Like welcoming not one, but two tiny balls of fluff into your home—and eventually into your heart.

Zeus and Cleo weren't just pets. They were our family. And when they passed, they took a piece of us with them, but also left a whole lot of joy behind.

So let me ask you this:

- Why do we wait to express our gratitude until it's too late?
- Why do we forget to appreciate the everyday magic we live with?
- And why does it take loss to remind us of how deeply we loved?

Everyone will answer these questions in their own way. But for me, the answer is simple: Love and gratitude must be practiced daily.

Let your people know you love them. Let your pets know. Say it out loud. Give the belly rub. Share the bacon.

Because at the end of the day, what matters most is how we *loved*.

So, here's to Zeus and Cleo—our little legends. You were quirky, cuddly, and sometimes chaotic. But you were ours. And we will love you... always.

FIVE SIMPLE WAYS TO SHOW LOVE & GRATITUDE —INSPIRED BY OUR FURRY ANGELS

Whether you're loving a partner, a pet, a friend, or yourself, love is best when it's shown, not just felt. Here are five meaningful ways to express love and gratitude in your daily life:

1. SPEAK IT OUT LOUD

Say "I love you." Say "I appreciate you." Say it often and mean it. Don't wait for birthdays, anniversaries, or goodbyes. Speak your heart today—even if it's to a picture frame, a paw print, or the empty spot on the couch where love used to sit.

Pro tip from Zeus: Say it before breakfast. Bacon tastes better with love.

2. CREATE RITUALS OF CONNECTION

Light a candle. Set a picture on your desk. Keep a journal of little moments you're grateful for purrs, hugs, laughter, even the quirky things that used to drive you nuts but now make you smile. Rituals keep memories alive and strengthen the bond we still have with those we love.

Cleo-approved tip: Make lap time sacred. Whether it's five minutes of cuddles with your cat or a quiet coffee chat with a loved one, be fully present.

3. GIVE THE GIFT OF TIME

Whether it's quality time with a friend, a game of fetch with your dog, or just sitting on the floor with your cat while they do *absolutely nothing*—time is one of the greatest gifts we can offer. Be generous with it.

Bonus tip: Phones down. Hearts open.

4. CELEBRATE THE EVERYDAY MOMENTS

Don't wait for big milestones. Celebrate the nap in the sun, the silly face someone made, or the way your pet used to snore louder than your spouse. The little moments *are* the big ones.
Start a gratitude jar—add one note each day about something (or someone) that made your heart smile. Revisit them when you need to feel loved.

5. KEEP LOVING—EVEN THROUGH LOSS

Grief is the price of love, but gratitude is the gift that remains. Continue to talk to them. Celebrate their birthday. Donate to a shelter in their name. Share stories. Love never leaves—it transforms.

Zeus and Cleo taught me this: Just because someone is gone doesn't mean love ends. In fact, sometimes it grows even deeper.

A LOVE THAT LINGERS

Grief is love with nowhere to go—but when we allow ourselves to feel it, to honor it, and to express it, that love does go somewhere. It becomes part of who we are. It deepens our compassion, softens our hearts, and teaches us how to cherish the living even more.

The love I have for Zeus and Cleo didn't end when their paws left the earth. It transformed into an invisible thread that connects us across space and time. It's in the stillness. The warmth of a sunbeam. The soft rustle of fur I swear I felt against my leg. Love is never lost; it simply changes form.

And here's the part that might just make your heart smile: I believe our pets are never really "gone." They just get promoted to *guardian fluffballs*, watching over us from somewhere just out of sight, occasionally knocking something over to say, "Hey, I'm still here."

So, if you ever find a toy you swear you packed away, or a whisker where there shouldn't be one, or if your blanket shifts when no one's around, don't be spooked. It's just a whisper from beyond:

"I love you. I never left. Thank you for being mine."

EILEEN E. GALBRAITH

With an innate talent for connecting with others, Eileen champions a philosophy rooted in dialogue, believing fervently that communication is the linchpin of a better world. Throughout her journey, mentors consistently hailed Eileen's joy in service, her intuitive grasp of people's desires, and her aversion to conventional sales tactics. For Eileen, sales were never about coercion; they were about understanding needs and offering solutions with sincerity and empathy.

However, it was adversity that propelled Eileen into the realm of entrepreneurship. Confronting personal crises, she discovered a reservoir of resilience and empathy within herself, prompting her to extend counsel to other women facing similar challenges. Thus, her accidental foray into entrepreneurship birthed two ventures in the early 2000s, now united under a single banner. Today, Eileen is not just a sought-after speaker and multi-time Amazon Bestselling Author; she is the visionary behind "Implement to Impact," a coaching enterprise dedicated to empowering women entrepreneurs with a focus on fostering time freedom, wealth creation, and a supportive community.

Author's Website: *www.ImplementToImpact.com*

Book Series Website: *www.TheBookOfFrequency.com*

GENESIS GOMEZ

CHOOSING GRATITUDE EVEN WHEN LIFE FEELS UNFAIR

There were seasons of my life where love felt like a distant concept—something reserved for other people with easier roads and softer landings. Gratitude, too, seemed like a luxury for those who hadn't walked through fire.

Yet somehow, through brokenness and rebuilding, I learned that gratitude isn't something you feel after the storm passes—it's the anchor that keeps you steady during it.

I didn't find love in picture-perfect moments. I found it in survival. I found it in my own resilience. In the tiny, determined hands of my children reaching for mine when I felt like I had nothing left to give. In the unexpected kindness of strangers who showed up when people I thought would stay chose to walk away. And most importantly, I found it within myself, in the stubborn whisper that refused to let my story end in bitterness.

There was a time when my life looked nothing like the dreams I carried as a little girl. I was a single mom, working multiple jobs just to keep a roof over our heads. The idea of pursuing passions like modeling or speaking on stages felt like a fantasy I couldn't afford. Every dollar was spoken for. Every hour was survival.

And yet, every night when I tucked my kids into bed, exhausted and worried about the next bill or broken promise, I still whispered, "Thank you." Thank you that we're here. Thank you that, somehow, we made it through another day.

Gratitude taught me to see beauty where others might only see brokenness. It showed me that love wasn't some grand, sweeping movie moment—it was the quiet endurance of staying, trying, showing up, even when no one clapped, even when no one noticed.

Later, when opportunities finally started to open—when I walked runways, won awards, and saw my face on billboards —people celebrated the visible success. What they didn't see were the countless nights behind the scenes, nights spent fighting self-doubt, healing invisible wounds, and choosing gratitude for progress even when perfection felt far away.

Love found me again, but not through someone else saving me. It came when I saved myself, when I decided to become the kind of person I had needed all along—for my kids, for my community, and for the younger version of me who almost gave up.

Gratitude became my way home. It wasn't about pretending everything was perfect. It was about noticing what was still good, even in the middle of the hard parts. It was about loving the parts of my journey that didn't go to plan because they shaped the woman I am today—strong, soft, steady.

Today, when I speak to women who feel like they're drowning, I tell them the truth: You don't have to wait for the storm to end to be grateful. You don't have to wait until you're "there" to choose love. You can begin right where you are, even with shaky hands and a breaking heart.

Gratitude isn't just something we feel when life is easy—it's a radical act of resilience when life is hard.

And love? It's not a prize we earn by being perfect. It's a birthright. It's something we learn to cultivate within ourselves —and then share freely with others.

This is the gift I carry now—not a perfect life, but a grateful heart. In that gratitude, I have found a richness no amount of hardship could ever take away.

I don't have all the answers, and I've never lived a perfect life. But I do know this: Love and gratitude have carried me through what survival alone never could. And every time I choose them—even now—I'm not just surviving. I'm becoming.

GENESIS GOMEZ

Genesis Gomez is a speaker, author, entrepreneur, and the founder of Reigning Resilient Queens, a movement committed to helping women rise through life's hardest chapters with strength, self-worth, and vision.

With a career spanning the worlds of modeling, public speaking, financial services, and end-of-life planning, Genesis brings compassion and clarity to every space she enters. Her journey reflects what it means to rebuild, to lead with heart, and to use every experience—personal and professional—as fuel for a deeper purpose.

Featured in national media and recognized for her authentic voice, Genesis continues to empower others to grow forward with grace and grit.

Author's Website: *www.GenesisGomez.com*

Book Series Website: *www.TheBookOfFrequency.com*

JAMI LAH

CREATING JOY ONE ENCOUNTER AT A TIME

Every morning, as the sun peeks through our bedroom curtains, I hear the gentle click of our Bose speaker turning on. Within moments, uplifting songs fill our home, a daily ritual that my husband, Chris, lovingly orchestrates to start our day on a positive note. This simple act of kindness is just one of the countless ways we tune into the frequency of love and gratitude that guides our lives.

I've always believed that gratitude is like a radio dial; when properly tuned, it connects us to a frequency that transforms ordinary moments into extraordinary ones. Throughout my life, I've discovered that this frequency isn't just accessible during life's grand celebrations but is available in every encounter, smile, moment, and opportunity that life offers me.

FINDING THE RIGHT FREQUENCY

"Keep smiling; people will wonder what you've been up to." This phrase has become my personal mantra. There's something magical about carrying joy with you; it creates a ripple effect that touches everyone in your path.

Of course, tuning into a high frequency isn't always easy. Life, with all its beautiful chaos, often brings static and interference. During particularly challenging times, I developed a practice that continues to serve me well: I pause and ask, "Am I doing this out of love or fear?" This single question works like a tuning fork, helping me recalibrate my actions and mindset toward clarity and purpose.

When obstacles inevitably appear, I've also learned not to resist but to adjust. I ask myself:

- "What new approach could I try?"
- "Where is there an opportunity to grow?"

Changing the questions can often change the outcome. This perspective shift is like adjusting an antenna to receive a clearer signal, one that ultimately connects me more deeply to what matters most: family.

THE FAMILY FREQUENCY

This journey toward gratitude began with my first teachers, my parents, affectionately known as Nana and Pops. They established a powerful legacy by demonstrating that nothing takes priority over family. They were always there for my sister, brother, and me, and later embraced their role as grandparents to my children with the same unwavering commitment.

Their example taught me that love isn't just a feeling but a frequency we choose to broadcast daily through our actions and priorities—a lesson I've carried into my own parenting journey.

Today, I'm profoundly grateful for my beautiful children, Jordan, Carly, Michael, and Michael's wife, Grace. Watching them grow and create their own lives fills me with a joy that words can barely capture. Finding love again with Chris has opened a new chapter filled with possibilities I never imagined, possibilities that led us to create something meaningful together.

A SHARED MISSION

When Chris and I married, we wanted our relationship to be more than just about us. We envisioned creating something meaningful together, a mission statement that reflected our shared values and guided our interactions with the world.

After thoughtful consideration, we landed on something beautifully simple yet profound to us:

Creating joy and reducing loneliness one person at a time.

Like many well-known brands with powerful mission statements—think Ben & Jerry's: *"To make the best ice cream in the nicest possible way"* or think Patagonia: *"We're in business to save our home planet"*—we wanted our personal mission to be actionable and authentic.

We realized we had countless opportunities each day to tune into this frequency, not just in planned charitable activities but in everyday moments. Our mission doesn't require elaborate planning or financial investment. It's about being intentional with each interaction, recognizing that every encounter offers an opportunity to broadcast on the frequency of love and gratitude.

SMALL ACTS, BIG IMPACT

This intentionality manifests in unexpected ways. One evening after attending a catered event, we noticed trays of sandwiches about to be discarded. Instead of walking away, we asked if we could take them. On our drive home, we took a detour downtown and distributed them to people experiencing homelessness. The gratitude in their eyes reminded me that sometimes the most meaningful connections happen in unexpected moments.

We've incorporated countless small practices into our daily lives: holding doors open for strangers, helping someone return their grocery cart, bringing cookies to gate attendants at the airport, offering genuine compliments freely, learning servers' names instead of saying, "Hey you," asking people about their families and backgrounds, inviting someone who might be lonely to join us for a movie or meal, taking five minutes to call an elderly friend or relative.

These may seem insignificant, but I've witnessed how these small kindnesses can shift someone's entire day, sometimes their entire outlook. It's like sending out a signal on the frequency of love and watching it bounce back multiplied, especially when we add an element of playfulness to our approach.

PLAYING ON LIFE'S FREQUENCY

Chris and I believe in the power of playfulness as another dimension of the love frequency. We create fun, positive videos for friends, family, and our broader community, designed to simply make people smile. We bring backgammon, cards, or Rummikub to restaurants and bars, setting up games that often intrigue others and lead to unexpected connections.

These playful moments tune us into a frequency of joy that transcends the ordinary. Like Sony's mission to "Fill the world with emotion, through the power of creativity and technology," we aim to fill our world with positive emotions through creative connections and simple technologies of human kindness.

This playfulness isn't just about entertainment; it's about creating a ripple effect that extends far beyond the initial interaction, much like the principle of karma that guides so many of our decisions.

THE KARMIC FREQUENCY

I strongly believe in karma and the concept of karmic debt, that the energy we put into the world eventually returns to us. Being kind costs nothing yet yields immeasurable returns. Like Starbucks' mission, "To inspire and nurture the human spirit, one person, one cup, and one neighborhood at a time," we've made it our mission to nurture individual human connections, one smile, and one community at a time.

This belief in karma isn't about expecting immediate rewards for good deeds. Rather, it's about recognizing that when we broadcast on the frequency of love and gratitude, we contribute to a collective energy that ultimately benefits everyone, including ourselves. It's a principle that requires daily practice and intention.

TUNING IN DAILY

Gratitude isn't just a practice for special occasions; it's a daily practice that transforms ordinary living into something extraordinary. Each morning, as those songs play through our speaker, I take a moment to appreciate the blessings in my life, both large and small. This simple practice tunes me into a frequency where problems don't disappear, but they certainly become more manageable.

I feel blessed beyond measure, and while life hasn't always been easy, I've learned that focusing on gratitude shifts my perception from what's missing to what's abundantly present. This shift in perspective continues to guide Chris and me as we look toward the future.

BROADCASTING FREQUENCY

As we step into the next chapter of our lives, we're committed to broadcasting on this frequency of love and gratitude with increasing intention. We believe that souls evolve through many lifetimes in the journey we call "life."

Like Google's mission, "To organize the world's information and make it universally accessible and useful," our personal mission is to organize moments of connection and make joy universally accessible through small, consistent acts of kindness. It's a mission we believe anyone can adopt and adapt to their own circumstances.

CREATE YOUR OWN MISSION FREQUENCY

I invite you, whether you're single or part of a couple, to create your own personal mission statement. This powerful practice can transform the way you approach each day and every interaction. Here's how to begin:

1. **Reflect on Your Core Values:** What matters most to you? Is it family, kindness, creativity, learning, or something else entirely? Identify three to five values that resonate deeply.

2. **Consider Your Unique Gifts:** What do you naturally do well? What brings you joy when sharing it with others?

3. **Identify Needs Around You:** What gaps do you see in your community? Where could your presence make a difference?

4. **Craft a Simple Statement:** Combine your values, gifts, and the needs you've identified into a clear, actionable statement. Keep it short enough to remember easily.

5. **Test it in Daily Life:** Try living by your mission for a week. Does it energize you? Does it feel authentic? Refine as needed.

Your personal mission doesn't need to be grandiose. It might be as simple as "Bring calm to chaotic situations" or "Create beauty in overlooked spaces." What matters is that it resonates with your authentic self and guides your interactions with the world.

When I look back at the path that brought me here, I see countless moments where tuning into the frequency of love and gratitude transformed challenges into opportunities, strangers into friends, and ordinary days into extraordinary memories.

The beauty of this frequency is that it's available to everyone, at any moment. All it takes is the decision to tune in, to choose love over fear, gratitude over complaint, and connection over isolation.

In the end, that's what matters most, not the accumulation of things but the accumulation of moments where we've touched others' lives and allowed them to touch ours.

After all, when we're broadcasting on the frequency of love and gratitude, we're never truly alone—we're connected to something far greater than ourselves.

JAMI LAH

Jami Lah has been producing TEDx events since she founded the first TEDxSemesterAtSea in 2011. She is the Executive Director and Producer for TEDxStGeorge, as well as the producer of TEDxSanDiego. Jami creates immersive experiences that have amplified ideas, reaching millions globally. Through her Lifelong Learning Worldwide initiatives, Jami develops transformative programs focused on living a rich and meaningful life. Lifelong Learning Worldwide transcends borders to foster cultural immersion, create innovative educational experiences, establish meaningful connections, and explore the diverse geography shaping our global landscape. Jami serves on the Advisory Board for The Multarity Project®, forging partnerships that unite people around challenging issues. Multarity Thinking™ leverages AI-driven technology to analyze and map dialogue with symbology, generating deeper empathy and inspired solutions. Additionally, she develops strategic partnerships for Naqi Logix, a leading neurotechnology company advancing human potential. Her work consistently bridges diverse perspectives, technologies, and cultures to create experiences that enrich understanding and foster positive change worldwide.

Author's Website: *www.Jami-Lah.com*

Book Series Website: *www.TheBookOfFrequency.com*

JOANNA RUSSELL
FINDING GRATITUDE IN LOSS & HEALING

Grief is a complex and deeply personal experience. It doesn't follow a predictable path, nor does it arrive with a clear set of instructions. When my mum passed away, I found myself grappling with emotions I didn't expect. Our relationship had always been challenging—marked by misunderstandings, unspoken frustrations, and a gap between the connection I longed for and the reality we shared. And yet, when she died, the grief hit me harder than I could have imagined.

I was surprised by the depth of my sorrow. For much of my life, I had carried a quiet resentment for the ways our relationship fell short of what I had hoped it would be. But in the year before her passing, something remarkable happened: she was hospitalized for an extended period, and those months turned out to be the best times we ever had together.

HEALING THROUGH CONNECTION

When my mum first entered the hospital, I initially approached the situation with a sense of duty and a determination to have no regrets rather than hope. I visited daily and stayed many nights, not expecting much to change between us. But as her health declined, something shifted in both of us. The walls that had defined our relationship for so long began to dissolve. Conversations that once felt strained became easier. Moments that might have been tense were instead filled with surprising tenderness.

For the first time in years, we talked pretty openly about her life, her regrets, and even about our relationship. She shared stories from her youth that I had never heard before, and in doing so, I began to see her not just as my mum but as a person with her own struggles and dreams. In turn, I found myself letting go of some of the anger I had carried for so long.

Those hospital visits and 4 AM chats became sacred. We laughed together more than we ever had before, and there were moments when she would say, "Thank you for being here; I like it when you're here." It was during those times that I realized how much love had always existed between us, even if it wasn't always expressed in ways I understood at the time.

Though bittersweet, those months gave me something priceless: closure. They allowed me to see her through new eyes—to understand her humanity and recognize how much she tried to love me in the best way she knew how. That realization softened my grief when she died; it didn't erase the pain, but gave it meaning.

THE UNEXPECTED GIFT OF GRIEF

When she passed away, I thought that having those final months of connection would make saying goodbye easier. Instead, it made the loss even sharper. I grieved not only for her absence but also for all the years we spent at odds with each other—the time we lost when our relationship could have been different.

As the weeks after her death turned into months, gratitude began to emerge alongside my grief. I was grateful beyond belief for those final months in the hospital when we were able to bridge the gap between us. I was grateful that we had found a way to connect before it was too late. I was grateful that she allowed me to see her vulnerability and that she saw mine in return.

I also found gratitude in what her passing taught me about relationships and forgiveness. Losing her made me reflect on how often we hold onto pain or grudges without realizing how fleeting life truly is. Her death reminded me to cherish the people in my life while they are still here, to focus on love rather than resentment, and to seek understanding rather than judgment.

FINDING GRATITUDE AMIDST DIVORCE

Two years after my mum's death, I found myself navigating another significant loss: the end of my marriage. Divorce is its own kind of grief—a mourning of shared dreams and a life built together that no longer exists. It was an emotionally draining process, compounded by the weight of losing my mum so recently.

At first, it felt impossible to find gratitude in yet another devastating situation. My world seemed to be falling apart piece by piece, leaving me raw and vulnerable. But as with my mum's passing, time brought clarity—and with it, an unexpected sense of gratitude.

In both losses, I've learnt that healing begins when we allow ourselves to feel everything fully—the pain, the anger, and eventually, the gratitude for what was good amidst what was difficult.

With my divorce, gratitude came from recognizing what the experience taught me: a deeper understanding of myself, resilience in the face of change, and the opportunity to rebuild my life in a way that feels more authentic and truer to who I am now.

Divorce forced me to confront who I was without my partner, to rebuild my identity, and learn how to stand on my own again. It hasn't been easy, and there have been many days when it felt like I was starting over from scratch, because, in many ways, I was. Yet through this process, I have discovered a sense of growth and strength I never knew I had.

Gratitude also allowed me to see divorce not as a failure but as a transition—a necessary step toward living a more authentic life.

LESSONS LEARNED: GRATITUDE AS A BRIDGE

Both experiences—the death of my mum and my divorce—taught me that gratitude doesn't erase pain but can coexist with it in powerful ways:

* **Gratitude Softens Regret:** With my mum's passing, I initially focused on all the years we lost due to misunderstandings. But gratitude helped me shift my perspective toward cherishing the time we did have, especially those final months when we connected deeply.

* **Gratitude Fosters Forgiveness:** Whether you forgive someone else or yourself, gratitude creates space for compassion and understanding.

* **Gratitude Helps You Move Forward:** In both grief and divorce, there were moments when I felt stuck—unable to imagine life beyond the pain. Practicing gratitude reminded me of what was still good in my life and gave me hope for what could come next.

A NEW PERSPECTIVE ON LOVE AND LOSS

Looking back now, I see both losses not just as endings but as transitions—opportunities for growth disguised as heartbreaks. My mum's death taught me about forgiveness and connection; my divorce taught me about resilience and self-discovery.

One of the most profound lessons these experiences taught me is the value of seeing things from a different perspective. When faced with loss or hardship, our initial instinct is often to focus on what's missing or broken, but shifting our perspective allows us to see hidden gifts within even the most painful situations.

For example, losing my mum helped me appreciate not just our final moments together but also all the ways she shaped who I am today, even through our struggles. Similarly, divorce forced me to reevaluate what truly matters in relationships—not perfection or permanence but authenticity and growth.

This ability to reframe challenges has become one of life's greatest tools for healing. By stepping back from pain and looking at it through another lens—whether through journaling or reflection—we can uncover new layers of meaning that help us grow stronger and more compassionate.

Grief is never easy—it's messy and unpredictable—but within it lies an opportunity to find meaning if we are willing to look for it.

These experiences taught me that love, healing, and happiness rarely arrive as we imagine, but if we stay open, they often find us in the most unexpected ways.

As you reflect on your own experiences with love and loss, consider this: What moments can you find gratitude, even amidst pain? What lessons have your challenges taught you about yourself or others? By embracing both grief and gratitude together and shifting your perspective, we can transform even life's hardest chapters into opportunities for healing and renewal.

In every ending lies a seed of beginning—and within every loss lies a chance to find love again: love for ourselves, love for others, and love for life itself.

JOANNA RUSSELL

Joanna Russell is a Senior Executive Coach and founder of Ajile LLC, recognized for expertly blending traditional leadership development with holistic coaching to drive organizational transformation and strategic growth. With nearly two decades of high-level experience in the UK healthcare sector as a Specialist Senior Social Worker, Joanna distinguished herself by managing complex cases, navigating intricate legal frameworks, and overseeing significant budgets—demonstrating advanced business acumen and operational leadership. Her transition from senior case management to executive coaching marks a natural evolution in her commitment to developing leaders and fostering organizational excellence. Now based in the U.S., Joanna partners with high-achieving professionals to restore motivation, elevate performance, and enhance leadership effectiveness. She also leads peer advisory groups and has served as Director of Coaching for a personal development company, designing impactful coaching frameworks. Joanna's warm, relatable, and deeply empathetic approach guides clients through sustainable transformation, helping them reconnect with purpose, set healthy boundaries, and thrive at the highest levels of leadership.

Author's Website: *www.AjileLLC.com*

Book Series Website: *www.TheBookOfFrequency.com*

DR. JOEL PARKER

SEIZING LIFE'S WAKE-UP CALL

The Oxford Dictionary defines gratitude as "the quality of being thankful; readiness to show appreciation for and to return kindness." It's a simple yet profound concept—a preface to the story I'm about to share, one that shaped my understanding of gratitude as both a mindset and a lifeline.

A ROUGH BEGINNING

My tale begins in 1974, in the uncertain months following my high school graduation. It was a tumultuous time, marked by the confusion, loneliness, and newfound independence that often define youth. My family had relocated from Canada to Australia just four months earlier, a move I chose not to join. At seventeen, I opted to stay behind and finish my senior year, a decision that might seem unusual but made sense amid the tension that had long simmered between me and my father.

He was a scientist, a man who challenged everything I said, especially when it veered into the realms of religion or spirituality—topics I'd begun exploring as a depressed teenager seeking meaning. I'd stumbled across *Be Here Now* by Baba Ram Dass and dabbled in meditation, much to my father's skepticism. His mantra was that in science, "Something is only suspected to be true by the number of times you've tried to prove it wrong and failed." This relentless questioning spilled over into our daily life, creating a battleground of ideas that left me exhausted. So, when my parents announced their move halfway around the world, I stayed, crashing temporarily with a friend's family.

The first six months alone were brutal. Loneliness gnawed at me, and the loss of familial structure hit harder than I'd anticipated. To compound matters, my high school principal had dismissed my aspirations as "pipe dreams," mocking their validity. The phrase, "If you can dream it, you can do it," hadn't yet entered popular consciousness, although L. Ron Hubbard was likely discussing "postulates" around that time, his ideas hadn't reached me yet. I was adrift, unmoored, and soon faced a harsh reality: I had no money.

THE WEIGHT OF FINANCIAL PRESSURE

After graduation, I moved in with friends, only to realize my funds had evaporated. I can't recall why I hadn't foreseen this, but the stress of financial insecurity descended swiftly. With nowhere else to turn, I visited the local welfare office and applied for assistance. A day later, they called me to pick up a check—a lifeline, or so it seemed.

But here's where the story pivots, where gratitude emerges from an unexpected source: the mindset my family had instilled in me. Beyond food and shelter, my father had taught me how to *work*. A bit of a renaissance man, he loved building

—concrete walls, small structures, anything requiring hands-on effort.

When we'd moved to the countryside years earlier, he'd enlisted my siblings and me in his projects. I learned to mix concrete, split cedar roof shakes, cut boards, wield a hammer, and dig out stumps. He paid us a modest allowance, but my thirst for cameras and acoustic musical instruments outstripped it. Rather than handing me the cash, he offered opportunities to earn it—a fair wage for honest work. At the time, I didn't see the value in those lessons. Decades later, I would.

A TURN TOWARD PRIDE

That day, as I drove to the welfare office, something stopped me. I couldn't bring myself to walk in and accept the check. Instead, I kept driving, past the office, through the small town, scanning for construction sites. I spotted one, parked, and approached the contractor. "Can I clean up the site?" I asked. He must have sensed something in me—a flicker of determination, a work ethic forged by my father—because he hired me on the spot. The next day, I was handed a leather nail-belt and a hammer, working alongside the onsite carpenter to frame walls.

Over the next two years, I poured concrete, assembled foundation forms, hoisted plywood and gyprock, and framed roof trusses. Skills I'd once taken for granted became my salvation. They gave me not just income, but pride—the confidence to create a job out of thin air. I didn't know it then, but I was living gratitude, not just feeling it. Those childhood lessons, forced upon me by a father I'd often resented, had equipped me to stand on my own.

GRATITUDE IN RETROSPECT

Years later, during the 2021 pandemic, I reflected on my father's relentless challenges. What I'd once seen as criticism, I now recognized as a gift: a quest for truth that sharpened my own thinking. His scientific rigor had pushed me to question, to observe, to seek what was true for me. The principal's dismissal of my "pipe dreams" had done the same, sparking a resilience I hadn't known I possessed.

That resilience—and the pride and perseverance my father's lessons instilled—later fueled a defining moment in my life: my quest to gain acceptance into Veterinary College. Out of 280 applicants, only ten were chosen, and I was one of them.

That achievement, born of years of hard work and a refusal to give up, was a testament to the skills and mindset I'd once overlooked. Life's challenges, I realized, often masquerade as burdens until time reveals their worth.

This pattern repeated throughout my life. The habit of hard work—showing up, taking pride in my efforts, and keeping my exchange with others fair—became a compass through later struggles. Gratitude, I learned, isn't just a reaction to good fortune; it's a lens that uncovers value in what we've been given, even when it's disguised as hardship.

SIMPLE RULES OF LIFE

From this journey, I've distilled a handful of truths—rules to live by, clarified through experience:

1. **Gratitude Fuels Both Skills and Attitude:** Be thankful for what you've learned and how you choose to carry it. Skills get you started; attitude keeps you going. Together, they build a life.

2. **Question Everything, Embrace Curiosity:** Challenge what doesn't add up. Truth is what holds up under your scrutiny, not someone else's decree. And curiosity? It's not a killer—it's a hunter, catching opportunities others miss. Be grateful for a mind that wonders.

3. **Welcome Challenges, Reject Invalidation:** When your beliefs or dreams are questioned, lean in—they're chances to grow, to find creative paths forward. But never let anyone diminish your worth in the process. Gratitude turns critique into strength.

4. **Cherish the Gifts of Your Past:** Skills or lessons forced upon you as a child—however tedious then—can become your greatest assets. Look back with thanks for the grains of truth buried in your history.

5. **Create Your Future with Gratitude:** Dream boldly. Show up consistently. Work hard. Opportunities will meet you halfway if you're open to them. Be thankful for the chance to shape what's ahead.

6. **Preserve Pride Over Handouts:** Refuse free money when you can earn your keep. There's dignity in exchange, in knowing you've held your own. Gratitude for self-awareness keeps you grounded.

FINAL THOUGHTS

Gratitude isn't passive; it's an active force that reframes our past, steadies our present, and propels us into the future. My story—from a lonely teenager rejecting welfare to a man thankful for a father's lessons, and later a veterinary student defying the odds—shows how it can transform even the roughest beginnings into a foundation for something greater.

As you turn these pages, consider where gratitude hides in your own life, waiting to be claimed.

DR. JOEL PARKER

Dr. Joel Parker, a veterinarian since 1984, became a private practice owner in 1986. He grew his practice, guided by solid management principles, into a Standing Ovation Practice™ —a practice that delivered an above-and-beyond expected experience. He later founded Veterinary Endoscopy Solutions and Canine Equipment™. After fiftteen years, he sold the businesses and started Veterinary Practice Solutions in 2004, a veterinary management consulting firm, innovated with "Whiteboard Wednesdays" on YouTube, and early online webinars. In 2024, he launched Parker Business Systems (PBS), a boutique-style consulting firm specializing in transforming privately owned veterinary practices into Standing Ovations Practices™.

He, above all, leads a purposeful life, helping others achieve time and financial freedom.

He lives with his family between Clearwater, FL, and Vancouver, BC. He enjoys sports cars, great coffee, strumming a ukulele, and playing with his unique, small, weird dogs.

Author's Website: *www.TheStandingOvationPractice.com*

Book Series Website: *www.TheBookOfFrequency.com*

JON KOVACH JR.

THE FREQUENCY FORMULA: HIGHER POWER

We don't talk about frequency enough. But you can sense it. You can feel when someone enters the room and brings warmth, and when someone else brings tension. What if you could control that energy?

When I say "frequency," I'm talking about the energy your thoughts, emotions, and actions emit, similar to a personal radio signal that affects everything around you. It's the emotional current we project into the world.

I've always believed in energy—perhaps not in the manner some might stereotype, but in the sense that everything we do, say, feel, and think has an exponential effect. From frequency to vibration, and the highest form of those frequencies? Love and gratitude.

These two forces have played a monumental role in shaping the success of my life. They're not just feelings; they're a choice, a practice, and a daily repetition that we can either engage in or overlook. And the more I've consciously chosen them, the more clarity, peace, and actual results I've experienced—whether in my business, relationships, health, or happiness.

THE MONSTERS INC. THEORY

The Pixar movie, *Monsters, Inc.*, totally gets it. The story revolves around monsters who harness power by harvesting the screams of children. Fear fuels their society. But by the end of the movie (spoiler alert), they realize something much more powerful than fear: laughter.

Laughter becomes a new, more efficient source of energy.

It's kind of brilliant. This animated children's movie holds a profound truth. Pixar was not too far off. I've seen it in my own life—positivity consistently outperforms negativity. It's not just theory—it's frequency. The frequency of love and gratitude is exponentially more powerful than that of fear, hate, or anger.

MY BODY CAN'T HANDLE ANGER

I don't know about you, but when I get angry—furious—my entire body shakes. I can't form coherent sentences. It's as if this volatile, unsustainable energy is hijacking me. Some people can function well in that space; maybe it's due to experience or simply who they are. But for me, it's not effective. It's not natural.

169

That's why "love conquers all" rings so true in my life. When I lean into love—when I say, "I love you, I forgive you, and I'm grateful for this experience"—I physically feel the shift. The negativity fades. The fear dissolves. My mind clears. That's not just a poetic sentiment; it's real energy work.

Positivity doesn't just counteract negativity—it erases it. And it doesn't do it at a 1:1 ratio. I've always felt that love carries ten times the energetic weight of fear. Just like in *Monsters, Inc.*, laughter was worth more. Love is worth more. It powered more. It lasted longer.

Want to experience this for yourself? Pause and whisper three things you're grateful for—out loud. Let the tone shift your mood.

LIVING AMONG LOVE & GRATITUDE IN THE PHILIPPINES

One of the most transformative experiences of my life occurred when I lived in the Philippines from 2008 to 2010. I was working to spread positivity—knocking on doors, sharing uplifting scripture, and inviting people to community gatherings. I believed I was bringing happiness to others. However, what I discovered was that I had entered a culture already deeply rooted in joy.

Filipino people are deeply family-oriented. Their joy didn't depend on how much they had, but rather on who they had.

Often, they didn't have much. They lived in modest homes with very little money, but they had each other. That was enough.

Even more inspiring was how much pride they took in their work. Bus drivers? Proud. Nurses, doctors, tech workers, and street vendors? Proud. Work wasn't just a job—it was an identity. And with that pride came a deep-rooted gratitude. They didn't just appreciate their work—they celebrated it. Their families did, too. It created a collective vibration of love and gratitude.

That frequency hit me hard. Why do people with less seem to be happier than those with more? Perhaps it's because their frequency is already tuned to love, appreciation, and having enough.

YOUR MINDSET DETERMINES YOUR FREQUENCY

Let's get real—are you tired of feeling stuck, drained, or disconnected, despite having everything that's "supposed" to make you happy? That's a frequency issue.

Consider practicing gratitude if you possess wealth, resources, and success but still feel empty or anxious. Gratitude acts as a pattern interrupt. It breaks the cycle of negative energy and resets your vibes. Focus on what you have—your family, your health, and the ability to serve and make someone smile.

Gratitude opens the door to abundance.

I've faced plenty of adversity. Like anyone else, I've had moments when the negativity was overwhelming—moments marked by grief, loss, betrayal, or fear. Those moments can be paralyzing. But the instant I remember that I can choose love and gratitude, it's like flipping a switch. It's not fake—it's intentional.

Some people worry about being disingenuous when they try to "snap out of it." But authenticity isn't a feeling; it's a decision. If I choose to act with gratitude, I'm being real. I'm not faking it —I'm redirecting, and that's powerful.

You can try this at home. Before going to bed, write down five things you're grateful for tonight. Don't just list them—breathe them in as you think of them and feel them.

NATURE'S FREQUENCY

Where else can you feel this frequency the most? Nature.

Barefoot in the grass. Toes in the sand. Feet in the flowing water. Breathing in the air during a sunrise hike. I know it might sound "woo-woo"—but it's real. The Earth has energy. I believe that. There's something sacred about grounding yourself—literally—with the soil and the energy of nature.

It has been demonstrated through science, spirituality, and ancient traditions that the Earth's energy can balance our own. When I take my shoes off and feel the sand beneath my feet during a game of sand volleyball, I feel recharged. It's more than just a sport. It's the transfer of energy.

Sand volleyball has become a spiritual practice for me (yes, really). I'm obsessed with it. My friends know it. My social media knows it. It's all I talk about outside of work and family. And I've realized it's because it aligns me with my highest frequency. Every game is a dance of energy, movement, connection, joy, and gratitude, all while soaking up some sun and playing in the dirt.

Spend ten minutes barefoot outside this week. No phone. Just breathe and listen. Let the earth recharge you. You'll see what I mean.

SALES IS A TRANSFER OF ENTHUSIASM

Now, let's talk business.

As someone who has grown in sales and entrepreneurship, I've learned that success isn't about scripts or pressure; it's about frequency. One of my mentors, Erik "Mr. Awesome" Swanson, taught me something game-changing: *Sales is simply a transfer of enthusiasm.*

Think about that.

You're not selling a product; you're transferring your excitement, love, belief, and gratitude. That's the sale. That's the energy exchange. That's what makes people buy. Not just because they want what you have, but because they want to feel what you feel.

Everything shifts when you operate at a frequency of love and gratitude in sales. You're not pushing—you're inviting. You're not convincing—you're transferring energy. And that, to me, is mastery of frequency in business.

The next time you discuss your business, focus solely on sharing your enthusiasm. Notice how people respond differently.

INERTIA, SPIRITUALITY, & THE FREQUENCY OF FORWARD MOTION

There's this principle in science—inertia. An object in motion stays in motion unless acted upon by another force. I think emotions are the same. Once you're in motion—mentally, emotionally, spiritually—with love and gratitude, you build momentum. You stay in motion.

It becomes your default state. Your home frequency.

And when you stumble or are knocked off course (which you will), love and gratitude serve as your re-entry points, your gravitational pull back into alignment.

Whether through grounding with nature, shifting your mindset, playing outdoor sports, watching a sunset, or connecting with people who make you smile, it all brings you back.

Consider frequency as your power source. Now, I invite you, just for a day, to live as if that's true. Tune in. Love deeper. Say thank you out loud. Plug into what matters most.

MY DECLARATION OF FREQUENCY:

I choose love over fear.
I choose gratitude over lack.
I choose alignment over anxiety.
I choose to plug into the power source within me.

I'm neither a frequency scientist nor an energy guru. However, I am a human being who has experienced the transformative power of love and gratitude enough times to know it truly works.

I've experienced moments when negativity dominated my day, and those are some of the toughest memories to hold on to—not because they weren't painful, but because they've faded over time. Anger has a short shelf life. But the moments of love? The memories of deep gratitude? They're etched into me like a tattoo of memory.

I remember smiles. I remember laughter. I remember the joy of giving, forgiving, and simply being grateful for what is.

So, if you're reading this and looking for a way to reset, reenergize, and realign, start with gratitude. Start with love. Let those patterns interrupt your low moments. Allow them to be your inertia.

The frequency of love and gratitude isn't just a choice; it's a power source that can recharge you and provide an immeasurable, sustainable energy.

And you can plug into it at any time.

This is my lived experience with the frequency of love and gratitude. It's not a theory. It's my truth. And I hope it becomes yours, too.

JON KOVACH JR.

Jon Kovach Jr. is an award-winning and international motivational speaker and global mastermind leader. In his work as an accountability coach and mastermind facilitator, Jon has helped and coached thousands of professionals achieve their goals with his Irrefutable Laws of High Performance. Jon is the Founder of Champion Circle Professional Development Association. He is also the featured Mastermind Facilitator and Team Leader of the Habitude Warrior Mastermind and the Global Speakers Mastermind & Masterclass series.

Jon is a 28x National #1 Bestselling Author. He is a featured keynote speaker on *SpeakUp TV*, an *Amazon Prime TV* series, and a TEDx speaker, delivering his signature speech, "Getting Unstuck." Jon's motivational messages have been viewed by over 1 million people, and his voice has trended and been used by global brands on TikTok, YouTube, and Instagram, including: Red Bull, Michael Bublé, Powell Books, GoDaddy Studio, Canada's Wonderland Amusement Park, the LSU Cheer Team, and the NHL.

Author's Website: *www.SpeakerJonKovachJr.com*

Book Series Website: *www.TheBookOfFrequency.com*

JULIE DELGADILLO

THE FREQUENCY OF TRUST

BUILDING INTEGRITY THROUGH SERVICE, SELF-AWARENESS, & LOVE

In my world—both personally and professionally—everything starts with trust. I've learned that trust isn't just a feeling. It's a frequency—a vibration you tune into through consistency, integrity, and love. Once you begin to resonate with that frequency, everything else in life—gratitude, connection, leadership, empowerment—starts to flow more easily.

I work in the nonprofit world and witness how trust either fuels or fractures the relationships we build daily. Donors entrust us with their gifts. Seniors rely on us for their meals. My colleagues depend on one another to show up and deliver on our promises. This ecosystem operates on a single currency: trust. Without it, everything crumbles.

But trust doesn't stand alone. It's upheld by integrity.

To me, integrity is more than a virtue—it's action. It's doing what you say you'll do, especially when no one's watching. It's honoring your word in public when people applaud and in private when no one will ever know. It's the foundation of who you are; when you compromise it, you compromise everything.

My dad used to say, "You can dream, but don't quit your day job." He wasn't trying to crush my ambition—he was teaching me responsibility. If you want to achieve something big, you must show up, follow through, and take care of your commitments. That's integrity. That's trust in action.

LEADING WITH YOUR WORD

In leadership, words matter, but it's how we live them that builds credibility. Leadership isn't just about making decisions —it's about demonstration. I often remind my team to don't just talk the talk; walk the walk. Show others what it looks like to follow through. Be the example.

Whether meeting with donors or delivering meals, I carry the same approach: transparency, honesty, and follow-through. We once had a moment when a senior was expecting their meals, but something went wrong in our delivery chain. That moment felt like more than a logistical mistake—a breach of trust. We failed to live up to what we promised, and for someone who may depend on that one meal a day, that's not just a missed delivery. It's a missed connection—a missed opportunity to show love.

That's when I realized that trust is love. When we trust others enough to serve them, and when they trust us back, it's a form of gratitude. It's a recognition that we're all in this together. That kind of bond raises the frequency of everyone involved.

PRACTICING TRUST LIKE A MUSCLE

Trust and integrity aren't just professional traits—they're personal muscles. You build them through repetition. Through honesty with yourself. Through showing up even when it's hard. At first, it might feel awkward—like exercising after a long break. But over time, consistency breeds confidence. The more you show up, the more you trust yourself. And the more you trust yourself, the easier it becomes to keep showing up.

Even something as simple as saying, "I'm going to exercise," and then actually doing it is a small act of integrity. It tells your subconscious, "I keep my promises." And when you do that enough, you build the inner alignment that carries over into every other part of your life.

You start to feel congruent.

You start to feel empowered.

You start to vibrate on a frequency where love and gratitude naturally exist.

YOU'RE NOT LATE—YOU'RE RIGHT ON TIME

One of the most healing lessons I've learned through trust is this: You're not behind. You're exactly where you need to be.

It's easy to look at your life and think, "I should be further along by now." We create invisible deadlines—by thirty, I should have this; by forty, I should have that. But those timelines are illusions. When we start honoring the integrity of who we are and stop measuring ourselves by someone else's path, we realize that we're actually on time. Perfectly on time.

Especially when we keep the promises we make to ourselves.

That's the deepest trust of all—the one we build inward.

FROM SELF TO SERVICE: LOVE IN ACTION

I've found that real empowerment doesn't come from just doing things for others—it starts by being true to yourself. We can't pour from an empty cup. We must nourish our trust and self-awareness before being present for others.

In my life, I made a significant decision to change jobs—not because I wasn't succeeding, but because I needed to be closer to my family, home, and the life I wanted. That choice came with sacrifice, but it also came with clarity. I could feel my alignment strengthening because I was finally listening to what mattered most.

I've also learned not to apologize for wanting more—mainly when it's rooted in love and purpose. There was a time recently when I hesitated to pursue something I wanted because I feared judgment. But I realized that if I let judgment control me, I'm out of integrity with myself. I'm no longer living on my frequency—I'm living on someone else's.

So, I went for it. And even if I failed, at least I tried. That's trust. That's love. That's gratitude.

PASSING IT ON

If there's one thing I try to teach new team members or mentees, it's this: Don't be afraid to show up. Build relationships. Build trust. You don't have to sell yourself or convince people of your value. Just connect. Ask questions. Be open. Be real.

Sometimes, you walk into a room and don't even talk business —you connect with someone human-to-human. And that connection creates trust. It opens doors. It builds bridges. It lays the groundwork for everything else.

Most importantly, it teaches you to trust yourself. When you show up fully, even if the opportunity isn't meant for you, you might be the one to open the door for someone else.

That's the beauty of living at the frequency of trust: it multiplies. It turns into love. It becomes gratitude.

And that's when the real magic begins.

JULIE DELGADILLO

Julie Delgadillo is a confident, enthusiastic, witty, and sought-after passionate servant leader and mentor with over twenty years of experience in non-profit management, leadership development, and confidence coaching. Julie is the Director of Meals on Wheels and the previous Executive Director of Corazón U.S. & Mexico. Julie is a firm believer in leading by example and actively engages in developing community leaders. It's not uncommon to catch her rolling up her sleeves and wearing a tool belt to personally contribute to building homes in Mexico for deserving low-income families.

Julie's strengths and passions are rooted in empowering women to be confident in every area of their lives. Julie has personally coached and developed teens and women from around the globe, serving as an International Ambassador for the economic development of women. Julie is also a former International Beauty Queen and a long-time Hunger Relief Advocate.

Author's Website: *www.linktr.ee/SheConquersTheWorld*

Book Series Website: *www.TheBookOfFrequency.com*

JULIE JONES

HOW HEARTBREAK LED TO FINDING MY TRUE SELF & LOVING HER

I sat alone in my one-bedroom apartment, reflecting on the long day after we laid my father to rest. His funeral was in an east Texas town, two hours east of Dallas. It's where Mom and Dad moved to after Dad retired. Dallas was their home for over fifty-seven years. It's where they raised my brother and me and built their careers, and where I now live.

Dad was the last of my nuclear family to pass on. My only brother had passed just six weeks before Dad. His death felt sudden. Dad had been sick. My brother suffered from a hereditary lung disease, and he wasn't well. But we didn't expect him to go before Dad. Their passing so close together almost too much to process. Mom had been gone for ten years, but I still missed her every day. I felt like I was floating in space without a rope to tether me to Earth. I couldn't feel the safety of gravity to ground me to the security of my family. It was a strange feeling.

Eleven months earlier, I had gone through a divorce. With one stroke of the judge's pen, the life I loved was gone. My now ex-husband and I had spent ten years building businesses together. I immersed myself in them and loved every minute, but suddenly, the relationship had fallen apart, and we couldn't put it back together again.

And as if that weren't enough, my dog, my sweet Lab mix that we rescued four years prior, had died the month before the divorce was final. I was the one who had to take him for his final veterinary visit. He had Lymphoma. One morning, I woke up to find him struggling to breathe. His eyes were huge as he looked at me for help. I broke down into a full-on sobbing, ugly cry.

In that moment, I could hear my mom say, "Be strong for him. Do what you need to do to help him." So, I called the vet. He knew from the last visit that Harley didn't have much time. He was expecting my call and was so kind to us. I held Harley in my arms, stroking his ear as he took his last breath. Then, I returned to work so I wouldn't have to feel the emotions of grief and sadness.

That year felt like one punch in the gut after another. Each loss cut to the core of my soul. My dog, my marriage, my businesses, my brother, my father… my life as I knew it. All of the men who kept me grounded and whom I looked up to were gone in just twelve short months.

I cried more that year than I had ever cried. I couldn't sleep. I couldn't focus. The thoughts that ran through my mind were: *How am I going to go on? Who can I look to when I feel scared? Who will I call when I need to hear a familiar voice? Who will encourage me when I feel lost?*

My friends would ask me what I wanted to do and where I saw myself in a year. I couldn't answer them. To be completely honest, I didn't even know who I was, much less what I wanted to do.

I had spent a lifetime serving my family, my children, my career, my church, but I didn't serve myself. My identity was rooted in being a helper, a caregiver, a servant.

Somewhere during my childhood, I internalized the idea that wanting things for myself was selfish. That it was wrong to tell someone "no," or to push forward to reach a goal. It wasn't considered "ladylike" to speak up or to express what was on my mind. "Just be nice." "Don't create conflict." "Get along."

These were the well-meaning lessons my parents taught me as they tried to protect me in a complicated world. But what they didn't realize was that they were also teaching me to silence myself, to put aside my own needs, wants, and dreams, and to keep my emotions in check so no one would see what I was really feeling.

In the days and weeks that followed Dad's funeral, my grief became so deep that I stopped doing things that I used to do. I went through the motions of daily life. I went to work. I came home. I went to bed.

On the weekends, unless my children or friends specifically invited me somewhere, I stayed in bed. Even getting dressed felt overwhelming, and I felt empty inside. Completely hollow.

About a month after Dad's funeral, my boss called me into a meeting to check on me, set goals, and discuss my career path. She told me she wanted me to learn a new skill so I could do more in my role and for the company.

The old Julie, the version of me that had energy and ambition, would have said, "Heck yes. Let's go!"

But the sad, hollow version of me just couldn't. I didn't have the emotional capacity to learn something new. I didn't have the strength to be a part of a team that was growing and moving forward. I missed being an entrepreneur. I missed my life with my now ex-husband. I missed my father's advice. I missed my brother's voice. I needed my dog curled up in my lap.

How could I help a company grow when I had nothing left to give? How could I be a great team member when the family that had anchored me emotionally was gone?

The truth was, I couldn't. I was still afloat. That realization came to me over a weekend, and on Monday, I had to tell my boss that I needed to leave. For the first time in my life, I knew

I had to focus on *me*. My children needed me. They were grown, but they had children. I had grandchildren who wanted and needed a grandmother who was happy and fun. I HAD to heal.

My boss was amazing. She offered to let me take FMLA and as much time as I needed to get through the grief, but deep down, I knew that wouldn't be fair to my clients, to the company, and to me. I didn't know how much time I would need, and the company needed me now. So, I left the company. And for the next year and a half, I focused on finding myself again.

I wrote. I journaled. I went to counseling. I peeled back the layers of who I had been and started rediscovering who I could become. I went to new events. I met new people. I attended Bible studies and learned to talk to God again.

But the most important thing that happened was that I learned to love myself.

I learned that it's not selfish to pursue your goals. It's not selfish to say "no" when someone asks for your time or money. It's okay, *more than okay*, to ask for help. And it's okay to seek out new friendships and to reconnect with old ones.

The greatest lesson I learned is that we are all here for a purpose and that finding that purpose can be a lifelong journey. We will all experience love and loss, win and lose. Each experience becomes a part of our story. And we are never truly alone. God is always with us. When we allow ourselves to sit with our emotions and to feel them fully instead of running from them, we will see that real growth begins.

Finding myself took work, giving myself grace, and learning that change is inevitable. It's part of life. Loss is a part of life, but it doesn't have to define us. I found reasons to carry on. I learned to embrace the new role of matriarch instead of the "baby" of the family.

Learning to love yourself is the starting point for truly living in your purpose.

JULIE JONES

Julie Jones is a Dallas-based business protocol and etiquette expert, corporate trainer, and sought-after public speaker. A certified graduate of the renowned Protocol School of Washington®, Julie brings a unique blend of experience as both an educator and entrepreneur. She spent fifteen years in education before building and successfully selling a plumbing company—proving her ability to lead, teach, and build from the ground up. Her passion lies in addressing a critical gap in today's professional world: the development of soft skills. Julie believes that success requires more than degrees or determination—it's about building trust, communicating with confidence, and forming lasting relationships.

Julie now works with professionals of all ages to refine their business image and interpersonal skills. Her client roster includes major corporations such as American Airlines, JW Marriott, and Grant Thornton, as well as prestigious universities like SMU, Texas Tech, and Tulane. She also coaches student-athletes, emerging professionals, and high school leaders, preparing them to thrive in the modern workplace.

Author's Website: *www.TodaysProfessionals.com*

Book Series Website: *www.TheBookOfFrequency.com*

LADY JEN DU PLESSIS
FAMILY VALUES & ACCOUNTABILITY

Love and gratitude have always been the foundation of my life, even when I didn't realize it at the time. They are frequencies— energetic states that I've learned to tune into, especially during the most difficult moments. These vibrations shaped my family, my career, and my personal evolution. Looking back, I see the moments that defined my understanding of these frequencies—moments where I stood at the crossroads of hardship and love, of resentment and gratitude, and chose to move forward with an open heart.

BUILDING A FAMILY WITH PURPOSE

I grew up as an only child until I was thirteen, surrounded by thirty-six first cousins who had built-in best friends in each other. Though I had the presence of extended family, I still felt a deep sense of isolation. My father's alcoholism and my mother's verbal abuse created an environment where I had to learn self-reliance early on. I remember watching other families and wondering if love could look different—if home could be a safe space rather than a battlefield of emotions.

When my husband, Brian, and I started our own family, we made a conscious decision: We would create a home filled with love, unwavering support, and accountability. We wanted our children to know that family was not just about sharing a last name—it was about being present for each other, lifting one another up, and digging deep to resolve problems rather than sweeping them under the rug.

Our approach to family is deeply rooted in accountability. Some families weed-whack their problems, trimming the surface-level issues without ever addressing the roots. We dig deep. We confront, we challenge, and we resolve. It hasn't always been easy, but it has created a foundation that keeps us strong and connected.

THE JENNY WHO AIN'T GOT A PENNY FREQUENCY

When I was a child, I was given the nickname, "Jenny who ain't got a penny." At the time, I tried to laugh it off—I even carried a penny in my shoe to show people. But underneath the humor lay a seed of scarcity, a message that stuck: that I would always be poor, always less than. That I was destined to repeat the patterns in which I was raised.

One day, I came home and saw my dad holding a shotgun to my mom's head. I ran into a field, praying I wouldn't hear a gunshot. The gun never went off, but something inside me clicked. That day, I vowed I would never be like them. I would rise. I would prove I was worth more.

That drive stayed with me for years, fueling my achievements but also trapping me in a cycle of constantly proving myself. I wasn't living; I was performing. Only when I allowed myself to tap into gratitude—for the resilience, for the lessons, even for the pain—did I begin to feel real love—not the kind that performs but the kind that allows.

THE POWER OF PRESENCE

Brian and I both came from backgrounds where our parents were absent—whether physically or emotionally. I saw my father choose alcohol over family, and Brian's parents divorced and remarried each other multiple times, creating instability in his world. Neither of us had the parental support we longed for, but we found it in each other.

We decided early on that we would be present for every milestone, every moment that mattered. We attended every game, every recital, and every school event. We didn't want our children to feel like they were alone in their achievements or struggles. This commitment to presence has extended beyond just our immediate family—it's the way we show up for each other, for friends, for colleagues, and for the people we mentor. Love is an action, not just a feeling. And we express that love through showing up.

ACCOUNTABILITY: THE BACKBONE OF LOVE

In our home, accountability isn't just a buzzword; it's a way of life. Every member of our family understands that we hold each other to a high standard—not out of criticism, but out of love. Our son even has a saying: "Mom, accountability." It has become a mantra that reinforces our commitment to taking responsibility for our actions, choices, and the energy we bring to our relationships.

One of our family mottos is, "Some families weed-whack their problems—we dig out the roots." Root digging is hard. It's sweaty, uncomfortable, and requires honest confrontation. But we believe that it'll grow back if you don't pull a weed by its root. We've had to model that, especially to our kids' spouses, who come from families where problems are glossed over. At first, our intensity scared them. But we kept saying, "Stay. Stay with us. This is what real love looks like. We fight, we cry, we resolve—and then we eat dinner together."

One of the hardest lessons in accountability has come through forgiveness. I had to learn to forgive my parents, not because they necessarily changed, but because I refused to let resentment dictate my life. Brian and I have both had to navigate the complicated terrain of forgiving those who failed us while still maintaining the boundaries necessary to protect our peace. Forgiveness is an act of love—not just for the other person, but for ourselves.

HOLIDAY HEALING: REWRITING THE SCRIPT

I remember telling Brian, "I don't ever want a holiday where a turkey is thrown across the room, or a Christmas tree gets tipped over." He replied, "And I never want a holiday alone." That simple conversation set the tone for the kind of family we were going to be.

Every Thanksgiving, we take time to share what we're grateful for. Every Christmas, we focus on presence over presents. It's not about perfection—it's about connection. The rituals we've created aren't fancy but sacred because they come from a place of healing, intention, and choosing a different frequency.

THE FOUR OF US: A FAMILY FREQUENCY

Brian and I, along with our daughter Whitney and son Kirk, often refer to ourselves as "the four of us." There's something deeply rooted about our connection—it's more than love. It's resonance—a shared frequency.

Kirk and I are the thinkers, the strategists. Whitney and Brian are the feelers, the empaths. Together, we balance each other out. Our family unit is tightly bonded, not because we're perfect, but because we're committed. And that commitment creates a frequency that reverberates in everything we do.

My daughter calls Brian when she needs help with the house or the car. My son calls me to talk business strategy. We each know who to contact for what, and it's all part of this deeply rooted tether we've built. We're tethered to the same ship. No matter how far we drift, we're anchored in love.

LOVE IN THE FACE OF CHALLENGES

One of the greatest tests of love and gratitude has come through Brian's traumatic brain injury (TBI). There are days when it feels like I am caring for a different person than the man I married. His memory loss, frustration, and mood shifts create daily challenges, and there have been moments when walking away felt like the easier option.

But love—true, unconditional love—isn't about convenience. It's about standing firm in our commitment through sickness and health. It takes courage to stay and fight for the person you love when they can't fight for themselves.

In those moments, gratitude becomes my anchor. I remind myself of all the years of joy we've shared, the adventures, the laughter, and the unwavering support we have given each other. That gratitude fuels my strength. And though it's hard, I choose to stay. I choose love.

THE FREQUENCY THAT HOLDS US TOGETHER

Love and gratitude are not passive states of being; they are frequencies we actively choose to tap into. They are the forces that shape our relationships, our families, and our legacies. In our family, love isn't just spoken—it's shown. Through presence. Through accountability. Through the hard conversations and the even harder acts of forgiveness. We show love through standing by each other when it would be easier to walk away.

I am grateful every day for the life we have built—not because it has been easy, but because we have consciously created it. And that is the true power of love and gratitude: they are choices, and when we choose them, they elevate every aspect of our lives. They are frequencies that, once tuned into, become the soundtrack of everything we build and everything we become.

LADY JEN DU PLESSIS

A dynamic leader renowned for transforming powerhouse businesses into companies that run smoothly without the need for daily intervention by its leader, Lady Jen Du Plessis is known as The Team Building & Scaling Architect who boasts over forty years in finance and over $400 million in revenue generated. She knows exactly how to build wealth through strategic team scaling, sustainable systems, and high-impact leadership, and has helped over 8,000 entrepreneurs leap from practitioners to thriving enterprises to achieve the pinnacle in their business.

She is a celebrated 22X Amazon #1 Bestselling Author, podcaster, and TV host who delivers real transformation, not just fast profits, so her clients achieve both business success and personal fulfillment. She cherishes her life in the countryside, enjoying local wineries, ballroom dancing, humanitarian efforts, boating, and quality time with family.

Author's Website: *www.JenDuPlessis.com*

Book Series Website: *www.TheBookOfFrequency.com*

KIMBERLY STEVENS

JOURNEY OF ONE ROSE

. . . .

In January 1992, after my fifteen-day-old son Braden passed away due to citrullinemia, one of eight urea cycle disorders, I planted a yellow sweetheart rose bush in his memory. It was purposefully right outside our front door, so I could pour every ounce of my love and grief into something alive. I followed every rule I could remember from my parents' gardening lessons: perfect soil, precise watering, and disease prevention. "If my love had anything to do with it, this would be the most beautiful rose bush ever." However, despite my diligence, no blooms formed. I nicknamed it Charlie Brown because it reminded me of Charlie Brown's Christmas tree.

Regardless, I cared for Charlie Brown with a mother's devotion. Gardening gave my empty arms something to do. My heart was broken and my hands needed purpose if I was to survive this tragic loss. Charlie Brown was a tiny connection point to Braden, a way to nurture something even though I no longer had my child to hold. Emptiness and loss filled my life, and I wondered if my tears would ever stop, but I kept watering and nurturing anyway.

About four months later, I noticed Charlie Brown had produced a tiny green bud, and I allowed a sliver of hope to penetrate my scarred heart. On Mother's Day 1992, the rose bloomed. I stood in the yard and wept. The world didn't see me as a mother that year because I had no child in my arms, but when that single rose bloomed at just the right moment, I knew God saw me.

Just before Father's Day, another rose bloomed. I clipped it and put it in the refrigerator to be a surprise gift on Father's Day. It was a small, silent gesture that meant everything. Those two yellow roses felt like God's quiet way of letting us know He shared our pain. During that awkward year, friends and family didn't know how to acknowledge us on Mother's Day and Father's Day. But those roses settled it. We *were* parents. And through two yellow roses, God showed us that we were not alone.

Almost two years later, as we celebrated the upcoming birth of our daughter, Victoria Faith, we were surrounded by baby showers, gifts, and so much hope. Despite having a one in four chance of being born with citrullinemia, Victoria had been prenatally cleared of the disease, which made everything feel even more miraculous and hopeful. Even Charlie Brown joined our celebration. After months with no blooms, a new bud was forming. I just knew it was going to bloom on her "birth" day.

Torrey was born on November 19, 1993. We welcomed her home on a Saturday, but Charlie Brown didn't. His bud was still green and tightly closed. On Tuesday, we got the call: backup testing revealed Victoria had citrullinemia, the same rare, devastating condition that took Braden. We raced back to the hospital. It was a cruel déjà vu because I had just let my guard down to love my new baby girl. Now I was being told she likely wouldn't survive another week.

We learned it was *possible* to survive with citrullinemia, but Victoria would require meticulous, precise, and vigilant care. Just six hours without medication could send her into a life-ending or life-altering metabolic coma. We spent eleven days in the hospital on stabilizing IV medications that she would need frequently and learned how to (or attempt to) fight citrullinemia. When we were finally discharged from the hospital, I saw it: Charlie Brown was right on cue with a single yellow rose.

In that moment, I felt God speak through that rose: Victoria would live, and I would not be alone in my fight to keep my daughter alive. Yellow roses became a deeply personal reminder from God that He was fighting my hardest battles alongside me.

I expanded my rose tradition: Each year, I give Victoria a pink rose for every year of her life to remind her of the same message: I see her, and she is not alone. As the bouquet grows, so does my gratitude. On January 1, 1995, as I watched the Rose Parade, I made a quiet promise to Victoria: One day, she would ride in that parade, surrounded by other children born with urea cycle disorders, carrying our family's rose-filled message of hope to the world.

I've never stopped seeing yellow roses.

Every Mother's Day and every year on Braden's birthday, no matter where I am, a yellow rose finds me. Sometimes it's a flower, a card, or a storefront display. No matter what form they are in, each time I see one, I'm reminded that God sees me, and I am not alone.

In 2023, Victoria turned thirty. I gave her thirty pink roses to mark the milestone, but I knew that wasn't enough. I had to do something bigger to match the depth of my gratitude for her miraculous life and everything still ahead.

That's when I started Extend the Rose.

Extend the Rose was born out of gratitude for Victoria's life and for the miracle of Braden's diagnosis that helped save her.

It exists to bring that same kind of hope to children and families in hospitals. We show up in the moments that feel forgotten and offer a compassionate interruption, just like those yellow roses did for me. Sometimes, we bring connection through a photo booth, our ROAR gallery, or lunch and laughter. However, the real gift is the message behind it: You are seen, you are heard, your story matters, and we celebrate YOU!

Each rose we share is like one Charlie Brown bloom reaching out to bring visibility, voice, and victory to children and families in the hospital.

This year, it's all coming full circle.

What began in 1992 as one yellow rose of hope in my darkest hour grew into pink roses for every year of Victoria's miraculous life. The gratitude I felt for that single bloom, and for the gift of her life, has never stopped growing. Today, that same gratitude is reaching farther and blooming into something beautiful, bold, and brave…

On January 1, 2027, our Rose Parade float will carry more than just flowers; it will carry children whose lives have been affected by urea cycle disorders and a hope-filled message to twenty-eight million television viewers: You are seen, heard, and CELEBRATED—never give up!

Love and gratitude kept me from giving up despite a tragic loss and a devastating diagnosis. They are also the reason Extend the Rose exists. They carried me through heartbreak and healing, and now they will carry a message far beyond my own story.

One rose will become twenty-eight million in the Rose Parade because love persevered and gratitude kept going. Charlie Brown is blooming into something I never could have imagined… because gratitude doesn't stay quiet. It begins in one heart and grows with each heart it touches.

One grateful heart in response to a tiny rose can ignite a movement, awaken hope, and change the world!

KIMBERLY STEVENS

Kimberly is a results-driven keynote speaker who empowers teams to harness grit and gratitude to exceed goals and expectations. With a powerful personal story of resilience and a proven record of success, she inspires organizations to take small, consistent steps that lead to big, measurable outcomes. A record-holding collegiate athlete and award-winning insurance agency owner, Kimberly brings firsthand insight into the power of determination, adaptability, and strategic action. Her career began with 16 years in pharmaceutical sales, helping patients navigate insurance complexities. Since launching her agency in 2016, she has helped individuals and businesses secure financial and health protection, reinforcing her belief that preparation and perseverance drive success. Kimberly's impact goes beyond business. She has transformed personal adversity—including the loss of her son, her daughter's life-threatening illness, breast cancer, and financial hardship—into a resilience formula teams can use to stay focused and push through setbacks. She is also the founder of Extend the Wave, a nationwide movement offering hope and encouragement to children and families in hospitals, ensuring no one faces their journey alone.

Author's Website: *www.KimberlyJStevens.com*

Book Series Website: *www.TheBookOfFrequency.com*

LATONYA AUZENNE
THE FREQUENCY THAT SAVED ME

I was not born into a life of ease or safety. I grew up in a house where love was missing—where survival was the unspoken rule and silence was a shield. There were no soft places to land, no gentle hugs, no warmth that wrapped itself around you and said, "You matter."

There weren't just birthdays or Christmases—there was no *love*.

What filled the space instead was chaos, neglect, anger, and confusion.

The kind of darkness that hums in the walls and gets into your bones.

Other people in that house vibrated at a frequency of fear, frustration, and emotional starvation—and as a child, I unknowingly began to match that frequency.

I didn't know any better. I thought that's what life was—that pain was normal. That love was a myth. That trust was dangerous. That low vibration became the background music of my early life.

And like a radio left on the wrong station, I learned to adapt to the noise, even though my soul longed for something sweeter.

THE QUIET ACHE FOR SOMETHING MORE

Even as a little girl, I would often press myself into corners, trying to disappear. I wanted to be invisible—not out of shame, but as a survival mechanism. If they didn't see me, maybe they wouldn't hurt me. Maybe I'd be safe.

Tears were my only consistent companion. They showed up more faithfully than any adult. I cried in silence, tucked away in closets or under blankets, hoping the pain would pass like a storm. But it never did. It lived with me.

It wasn't until many years later that I held Iyanla Vanzant's *Yesterday, I Cried* in my hands—and felt the dam inside me burst.

That book mirrored my soul.

I wasn't alone.

I wasn't crazy.

And I wasn't broken beyond repair.

Iyanla wrote, "The soul always knows what to do to heal itself. The challenge is to silence the mind."

For me, the mind was filled with static—beliefs I inherited from trauma.

But my soul? My soul remembered something sacred. My soul remembered *love*.

ASKING THE UNSPOKEN QUESTIONS

Years before my mother passed, I found the strength to ask her the questions that haunted me, the questions I had buried deep to avoid the pain of the answers.

"Mama, what was wrong with Grandma?"

Her eyes lowered. Her voice cracked.

"She was diagnosed with paranoid schizophrenia," she whispered. "She spent most of her life in and out of mental hospitals."

Suddenly, my childhood made more sense.

The unpredictability.

The fear.

The emotional absence.

But it didn't stop the ache that came with my next question, "Why did you leave me with her?"

That answer came with tears.

"Tonya, God has something special for you."

And in that moment, I understood something deeply spiritual: Sometimes, your pain is the path.
Sometimes, the ones meant to protect you fall short—not out of malice, but out of their own brokenness.

Forgiveness didn't come instantly, but that moment cracked the door open. Not because the pain vanished, but because I chose to rise above it.

Forgiveness became my personal declaration: I am not what was done to me. I am what I choose to become.

THE TURNING POINT: DISCOVERING A NEW VIBRATION

One day, years after that conversation, I picked up Napoleon Hill's *Think and Grow Rich*. It didn't just speak to my intellect —it activated my soul.

Hill wrote, "Every adversity, every failure, every heartache carries with it the seed of an equal or greater benefit."

I read that line again and again, letting it pour into the cracks of my story. Could my pain carry a purpose? Could my suffering hold seeds of greatness?

That idea awakened something inside me—a different frequency. A vibration that whispered, "There's more for you. But you must tune in to it."

Napoleon Hill taught me that my thoughts were not just reactions—they were creations. And if I could think differently, I could live differently.

LOVE & GRATITUDE: THE FREQUENCY SHIFT

From that point on, I made a conscious decision to rewire my vibration.
I didn't just want a better life. I wanted a better *being*.

That journey began with two powerful forces: Love and Gratitude. Love is not just a feeling; it's an energetic state. It's a way of showing up to life with openness instead of defense, compassion instead of control.

Gratitude is not just saying, "thank you." It's the decision to see every breath as a gift, every challenge as an opportunity, and every moment as sacred.

Together, love and gratitude create a frequency so high that it naturally attracts peace, people, purpose, and prosperity.

LOVE IS THE HIGHEST

What's beautiful—and often misunderstood—is this: The highest frequency doesn't look like being the loudest in the room.

It doesn't demand applause or seek validation. It surrenders. It serves. It listens. Love is the highest. Love kneels. Gratitude bows. And both elevate you beyond what you thought was possible.

When I began vibrating at the frequency of love and gratitude, I no longer needed life to "fix" itself. I started becoming the healer. I attracted better relationships and more aligned opportunities. Most importantly, I attracted a peace that could not be shaken by circumstances.

THE MIRACLE IS ME

Today, I wake up in a home where laughter echoes through the walls. I cook meals surrounded by family. I kiss my grandchildren on their cheeks and tell them they are safe, they are seen, they are sacred.

And often, I pause—not to remember the pain, but to honor the miracle: I became the love I didn't receive. I became the voice I never heard. I became the light I once longed for in the dark.

A CALLING BIGGER THAN ME

This frequency is not just for me. It is for everyone, especially those who were raised on survival and silence.

When I coach, speak, or share my truth, I'm not trying to impress—I'm trying to imprint and to remind others:

- Your pain is not your identity.
- Your past is not your prophecy.
- And your power is in your vibration.

I teach people to shift by shifting how they feel, think, and speak because what you speak affects how you feel; what you feel, you vibrate, and what you vibrate, you attract.

THE FREQUENCY THAT SAVED ME

If my life is a testimony to anything, let it be this:

"What the mind can conceive and believe, it can achieve."
~ Napoleon Hill

I didn't change my life by force. I changed it through frequency by aligning with love and practicing gratitude until it became my default setting.

I no longer chase miracles. I attract them—because I've become one.

So, if you're reading this and wondering if the frequency of love and gratitude can really save you, I'm living proof: **It can. It did.**

And it still does.

LATONYA AUZENNE

Latonya Auzenne is a purpose-driven entrepreneur, certified Napoleon Hill instructor, and NeuroChange Practitioner dedicated to transforming lives through mindset mastery and business empowerment. As co-owner of IRIDE Transportation, she helps deliver safe and reliable non-emergency medical transportation across Louisiana. Latonya is also a passionate speaker, author, and direct sales leader, using her voice and personal story to inspire others to rise above adversity and reclaim their power.

Raised in Shreveport and now rooted in Lafayette, she brings a deep commitment to faith, integrity, and community impact. Latonya serves as Secretary of the Greater Southwest Louisiana Black Chamber of Commerce, where she champions minority-owned businesses and economic equity. Through workshops, coaching, and public service, she equips others with the tools to live their dreams and create lasting success. With a heart for healing and a bold vision for the future, Latonya is living proof that with belief and action, transformation is possible.

Author's Website: *www.CEOLatonya.com*

Book Series Website: *www.TheBookOfFrequency.com*

DR. LÉ SANTHA NAIDOO

SEEN: A LOVE STORY THAT BECAME MEDICINE

It was a late evening after a grueling sixteen-hour EMT shift. Though exhausted, I found myself at a party in our basement, clutching a soda and contemplating escape. Social gatherings had become a strange dance between my two worlds—the studious pre-med persona and the wilder EMT side my friends had introduced me to. That night, neither felt right as I watched others laugh and mingle with an ease I couldn't find.

That's when he appeared. Tall with curly hair and a little goatee, he looked more like an oversized teddy bear than a romance novel hero. He approached with a warmth that seemed to part the noise around us.

"Your hair looks really good," he said, his voice carrying a genuineness that caught me completely off guard.

I blinked, stunned. People didn't notice things like my hair. I was the smart one, the responsible one with life mapped out in meticulous checklists. I wasn't used to being seen for anything else. "I love how full and bouncy your hair is," he continued, smiling. "It's just perfect for your personality."

Something shifted in that moment—a feeling I wouldn't understand until years later. When we experience genuine love and appreciation, our bodies respond by vibrating at a higher level. The heart produces a measurable electromagnetic field that changes pattern when we move from stress to love.

That night, standing before this stranger who somehow saw me, I felt that shift beginning. He became interested in me— not in my achievements or my plans, but in me. He wanted to know my dreams, my passions, the person behind the ambition. As we talked, layers of tension I hadn't even realized I was carrying melted away. For the first time in forever, I wasn't performing or pretending. I was just being.

Hesitant and confused, I let him take my hand when he asked me to dance. These simple gestures created a frequency between two human beings that transcended the ordinary.

Our connection deepened over the following weeks. He challenged me to try new things, to see life from different angles, to step beyond the rigid boundaries I'd constructed. He was simultaneously goofy and serious, funny and worldly in ways that fascinated me.

What amazed me most was how he saw me at my worst— literally. I'd stumble in after a long shift on the ambulance, covered in sweat, exhaustion, and questionable substances from the day's chaos, yet his eyes would light up like I was the most radiant person in the room. He made me feel beautiful even when I looked like I'd been through a war zone. His quiet voice, his gentle touch, and his presence brought peace to the chaos of my days. He made room for all of me.

I didn't know then that being truly seen by another person creates one of the most powerful healing frequencies we can experience. When someone reflects our value without condition, it rewires something fundamental in our nervous system. The constant vigilance relaxes. The need to prove our worth subsides. Our fight-or-flight response calms. This happens not just when we're loved by another, but when we love them back—or even when we love ourselves.

Then came the rumors—whispers that reached him and eventually my brother. I never knew exactly what was being said, but it was apparently damaging enough to threaten what we'd built. One day, he sat me down, his expression serious yet gentle. "Lé Santha, we need to end this," he said, his voice steady but laced with sadness. We can't see each other anymore."

Before I could process the shock, he continued, "There are things being said about us, and I can't let that tarnish your reputation. You're going to be an amazing doctor one day. You can't have a tarnished reputation before you even start. You're strong, beautiful, and capable of so much, and I can't be the reason any of that is jeopardized."

In that moment, I witnessed the highest frequency of love—one that transcends personal desire in service of another's highest good. He ended our relationship not out of anger but out of love and respect. He stepped away with dignity, defending me even as he let me go.

Strangely, I wasn't heartbroken. Instead, I felt empowered. Through his eyes, I had glimpsed my own worth in a new way. He believed in me so deeply that he was willing to sacrifice his own happiness to protect my path forward. I was grateful that he cared enough about who I am as a person to end the romantic relationship.

That experience changed everything. It was as if a door I hadn't realized was closed suddenly swung open. I felt more magnetic, more connected to the world. With each interaction that followed, I found myself experiencing not just love but profound gratitude for his presence in my life, his perspective, and the way he had made room for all of me. This combination of love and gratitude created a resonance that began transforming me from the inside out.

People began responding to me differently—or perhaps I was finally open to receiving the connection that had always been available. The vibration of worthiness that had awakened in me was attracting new experiences, new relationships, and new possibilities.

When we operate at the frequencies of love and gratitude, our bodies produce different biochemistry. Inflammation decreases. Heart rate variability increases—a key marker of cardiovascular health. Our immune system strengthens. We even age more slowly at a cellular level.

These aren't just poetic metaphors; they're biological realities I've witnessed both in my patients and in my own life. People who cultivate love and gratitude, even amid struggle, heal faster. Their bodies respond differently to treatment, and their prognoses improve.

That brief but profound relationship taught me that love isn't just an emotion—it's medicine. Gratitude isn't just an attitude—it's a healing force. Together, they create a frequency powerful enough to transform not just our mood but our molecular structure.

In my personal health journey, I've learned that vibrating in harmony with my own worth, potential, and capacity for joy elevates my frequency. It started with someone else seeing me, but it continued as I began to see myself through love and gratitude, rather than judgment.

LÉ SANTHA NAIDOO

A revolutionary force in medicine, Dr. Lé Santha Naidoo transcends traditional healthcare with her triple board certifications and visionary approach to wellness. As founder of Avyanna Wellness Institute and "The 100 Club," she delivers bespoke health optimization to an exclusive clientele, transforming lives through personalized and precision care. Rising from adversity to international acclaim, her journey to becoming a pioneering physician and her health advocacy captivate audiences worldwide on major television networks (*NBC*, *ABC*, *CBS*, *FOX*) and global stages. Her bestselling memoir, *Fat to Fabulous*, stands as a testament to her extraordinary resilience.

Receiving many honors for her community service, leadership, and ranking as America's Best Concierge Physician, Dr. Lé Santha's brilliance extends beyond medicine—she's a fierce mentor, philanthropist, and catalyst for human potential. Her unique blend of medical mastery and profound compassion creates not just physical healing, but profound life transformation.

Author's Website: *www.LeSantha.com*

Book Series Website: *www.TheBookOfFrequency.com*

LISA CANNON

ALCHEMY OF THE HEART: FUELING SUCCESS

· ·

"Reflect upon your present blessings, of which every person has plenty, not on your past misfortunes, which all persons have some."

~ Adapted from a Charles Dickens quote

What are love and gratitude? I asked myself how I was supposed to express love and gratitude in words to my readers. We can give love and receive love, but what is it? What does it look like and feel like? It's like electricity. You can't see electricity, but you know when it works through the results. A light goes on. It's working!

With the help of others, I asked, "How could I share what love and gratitude mean to me?" This is what I found.

When I was a very little girl, around three years old, my dad would put me on his shoulders when I got tired of walking. That was an expression of love. When I was sad or bored, my mom would engage me in making food. We made the best apple pies. I can taste the Macintosh apples right now. I would eat the leftover slivers of pie crust, dip my fingers in the cinnamon sugar, and savor slices of apple I grabbed from the pie plate. These are acts of love my parents shared with me.

I'm not sure if it was because I was the last of eight kids and my mom was just tired of disciplining kids or if she really knew my heart. She would let me eat as much or as little food on my plate—usually the latter. I was a super picky eater.

My auntie used to try to get me to eat "yucky" food. One day, I had to sit at the table until I finished. She would try to bribe me to eat it, such as telling me I couldn't play outside with the others until I finished. It didn't matter to me. I just sat there calmly and quietly. There was no way in this world I was eating that chili. I hated those red kidney beans. Nope, no way. She did this with love, of course. I was still sitting in the same chair when my dad came to pick me up, hours later.

Nothing was said; she picked up the plate, and my dad took me home. That was my aunt's way of expressing love. She wanted me to be nourished.

Fast forward to me developing into the person I am today. I had this innate intuition about people, things, ideas, food, and the world around me. I just knew the world was good, despite many unfortunate things that happened to us. I was a sunny, sweet, compliant child who just knew things.

My mom and I were driving to a town I had never been to, but she had many times. She went a new way and was a little lost. When we came to a T in the road, she said, kind of to herself, "I'm not sure whether to turn right or left?" I said, "Go left, then go down a bit and turn left. I'll tell you where."

She laughed and said, "What makes you think you know the way? You have never been on these roads before." I just knew, and I was right! My mom was quietly amazed. I heard her tell her friend this story. Her friend didn't know what to make of it; they both smiled, shrugged their shoulders, and tilted their heads.

I suppose my love is expressed through intuition. I know when strangers need a little chat in the grocery store or when a child needs to vent. I listen a lot. I watch closely. I notice that people often try to mask their feelings and true selves by "acting" differently from who they really are. Sometimes what a person does or says is completely incongruent with their true self.

Occasionally, people don't even know who they are anymore. At times, a stranger just listening to them talk is exactly what they need. That's where I show up. Sometimes I make people nervous because they share details of their lives or behaviors that they never revealed to anyone else, and they don't know why. I don't either. It is unintentional. I am just a vessel of love and gratitude. I have always seen the glass as half full. Even when I am boiling mad. Oh, it's irritating sometimes. I just want to be so angry, and then I realize I either needed to vent, needed to be a part of a frustrating situation, or to hear someone go on and on ad nauseum. So, I get my attitude straight and move on.

I am grateful for my innate intuition. It is a big part of who I am. It's also weird to be able to understand people at a deeper level than they even know themselves. I got to a point where I could hear chatter in people's minds. Whoa! That alarmed me. I thought, how far can this intuition thing go? Is it a skill? Can I grow it? What happens next? Do I start seeing dead bodies? I laugh at the thought.

Honestly, I love being able to help people and know people this way, but I share it sparingly. I use it in my coaching to help my clients achieve the success they seek. I'm not a mind reader, and I can't make things happen. That is the job of the client. I can guide using the knowledge clients share, and combined with my intuition and being in a grateful mindset, this method provides extremely valuable outcomes.

Have you heard of a gratitude journal? I came across the concept from an Oprah TV show episode. She talked about how useful it was for her, so I decided to try it. I wrote down five things I was grateful for every night before bed. However, I was a mom of a toddler, exhausted and craving a full night's sleep. The last thing I wanted to do was go to bed, pull out my journal, and write anything. I was exhausted. Did I mention I had a toddler? So, I was not very grateful for a gratitude journal. However, as my days progressed, I noticed that when I was grateful for things, people, and situations, I felt a sense of calm.

Take today, for instance. I was walking on a narrow sidewalk when an older lady, with a cane, hunched over, and an older gentleman were walking toward me. It gave me pleasure to step off the walkway onto the road so they could safely and confidently walk by me. I thought about how lucky I was not to need a cane or a walker. I smiled. I find noticing those special moments throughout my day makes me happier and more grounded than making lists. It works for me.

So... gratitude and love? When I examine them closely, I realize that both are intertwined and alive in me. I am lucky that way. How did I get this way? I have no earthly idea, but if I had to guess... I would say it's because I have good genes, respect for my elders, great listening skills, and a genuine curiosity about life. I'm intrigued by people and places. I love to travel on public transportation to get the local vibe, listen to and watch people, and interact if the occasion presents itself. The occasion, of course, is my curiosity!

Just this week, I had a big birthday—a decade one. I made some clear decisions about my life. After spending time away from home on two different work-related trips, I became clear about life. I am grateful I am still here, and I am more intentional about loving myself. I made these goals: Number one, focus on my health; number two, grow my business; and, number three, increase my attention toward intuition, which improves all of the above.

Now, ladies and gentlemen, a couple of final thoughts: "Life is ten percent what happens to you, and ninety percent how you react to it." Are you grateful? Could you be more grateful? What would life look like? Equally, are you a loving person? Could you incorporate more love into your life? What would your new life look like?

Many times, I have found that small shifts are important ones. Shifts in the way you approach life can change everything. Are you reacting with love and gratitude or something very different? It doesn't matter how you got here. It only matters what you do next.

If you are ready for change, please feel free to reach out. It would be my pleasure to meet and work with you to achieve your personal and/or professional goals! Cheers to your next step!

In love and gratitude,

~ Lisa

LISA CANNON

Lisa Cannon is the founder of 4SuccessU, a coaching and consulting company committed to helping women entrepreneurs build profitable, purpose-driven businesses. With over twenty years of experience in coaching, training, consulting, and public speaking, Lisa has empowered thousands of professionals to gain clarity, confidence, and direction through her signature blend of strategic systems, intuitive insight, and practical mindset tools. Having navigated her own share of personal and professional transitions, Lisa brings a deep, authentic passion for helping others step into their next level.

Her specialty lies in guiding clients through pivotal transitions—helping them shift from stuck to strategic, scattered to focused, and overwhelmed to thriving. Lisa's coaching style is straightforward and results-driven, yet always grounded in empathy. She's also a published author and widely respected for her no-fluff, heart-centered approach. Her motto? Life is short—show up boldly, lead with purpose, and become the greatest version of yourself.

Author's Website: *www.4SuccessU.com*

Book Series Website: *www.TheBookOfFrequency.com*

M.A. FULTS
LOVE PROVIDES

. . . .

FREQUENCY

My definition of frequency is based on electrical engineering, a dad who loved all things audio, and the fundamental idea: How many times something is repeated. Side note: Dad's idea of good music, often played in our house throughout the day, was classical symphony and opera. I came to appreciate both, though Wagner's operas not so much.

In electronics, the higher the frequency, the higher the number of repetitions.

TO LOVE IS A CHOICE

Love is not the "highest" form of *like*, although it is often used that way. How many times do we say or hear, "I love ..." insert a favorite food or entertainer, a type of music (I almost used the term above to say "I came to love both..."), or anything that is really liked? Wait, you might say, I really do "love" pizza! Do you, though? You enjoy and eat it often, but do you truly "love" it?

Love comes down to loving someone. How much you love them is evidenced by what you are willing to do for them, how you treat them, the impact they have on your life, and, at its most extreme, your willingness to lay down your life for the one you love.

I truly believe that loving someone is a heart choice. Love cannot be forced, coerced, or manipulated. Yes, your love can be used to force you to do something you would not do otherwise, but you cannot be forced to love someone or something. You must choose. I chose to love others a long time ago. I don't always live up to that, but I did decide that loving others, no matter what, was what I aspired to—mainly due to one thing: How much my God loved and loves me.

HIGHEST FORM OF LOVE

The highest form of love, with the highest frequency, is found in the Holy Bible in the first letter of the Apostle Paul to the Corinthians, the thirteenth chapter. Most have heard or read this list of love's attributes, and I've used The Passion Translation below.

A number of years ago, I received a suggestion to replace the word "love" with my own name. As you read through this list of Love's attributes, I encourage you to do the same.

Love is large and incredibly patient. I endeavor to be patient, a struggle in trying times or with trying people. It's not easy, especially when I see injustice against someone unable to fight for themselves. However, I continually remind myself that others don't "try my patience" because I am the only one able to control myself. Of course, its corollary is that I cannot control others; each one can only control themselves.

Love is gentle and consistently kind to all. Being identified as a gentle person is seemingly rare these days, but it is oh so very important. Gentleness allows for all, young and old, big and small, coordinated and uncoordinated, to be welcomed at the table and feast. Kindness is looking for the "have-nots" and willingly sharing what you have.

It [love] *refuses to be jealous when blessings come to someone else.* Sometimes, I have to tell myself to rejoice in the blessings others receive. The easiest way for me to accomplish this is by being a blessing, not just to family and friends but to all. Being a servant to all is another of my aspirations.

Love does not brag about one's achievements nor inflate its own importance. I've never been one to brag about myself, and usually, others have to coax out of me what I've done. Where I struggle is in accepting praise from someone else. I'm not sure I can call it humility; it's more like self-deprecation, which is not love. I'm a work in progress, here.

Love does not traffic in shame and disrespect... This is another area where I struggle. I tend to wear a coat of shame that is of my own making. I've learned that the shame comes from lies I've believed about myself. My head knows this, but my heart is being healed so that it can believe the truth spoken to and over me.

...nor selfishly seek its own honor. I don't think I've selfishly sought my own honor, though I'm appreciative when others have honored me. Again, I think my non-humble self-deprecation is more of a defensive redirection, because I continue to believe that I don't deserve the honor. Yet, honor is a good thing and should be given and humbly received. God honors us, and we are called to honor each other—and I'm working on that.

Love is not easily irritated or quick to take offense. I'm not usually easily irritated or quick to take offense, unless, as indicated above, I see an injustice, a wrong done to another, especially one incapable of finding justice on their own. That's not to say I haven't lost my temper or struck out at someone or something in anger. But, as with all of these attributes, I'm getting better at them over time.

Love joyfully celebrates honesty and finds no delight in what is wrong. Honesty? That has been my goal and methodology since my college days. I made the choice that I would always tell the truth. Lately, though, I have been learning that telling the truth, with love at its core, often means holding my tongue. Not everything needs to be said, even if it is true. As to "wrong," no, I've never been delighted to see a wrong done to anyone.

Love is a safe place of shelter, for it never stops believing the best for others. Love, when it's the core of what I do, when love is the only place I'm coming from... love has me listening to hear, speaking only with compassion, and keeping a "safe place" in both our hearts and minds. Positive mental attitude often leads to believing in the best of and for others. I tend to be positive most days and in most situations. I'm a firm believer that there is always an option.

Love never takes failure as defeat, for it never gives up. How many "self-help" gurus have you heard say this very thing? Failure is not the end; you learn more from your failures; failure is just another step to success; never let failure stop you —you may be only three feet from gold. I'm grateful that my failures have, eventually, led to successes. Though I have at times wallowed in the failure, it never became a defeat; my faith in a God who never leaves me, always loves me, no matter what, served to lift me up and bring me back to living. When I got back to my feet, dusted myself off, and moved on, I found love had sustained me.

Love never, not even once, fails. Never take failure as defeat. Love never fails. Yes! (*1 Corinthians 13:4-8a* The Passion Translation).

LOVE AS THE SOURCE

When love is the core, the root, and the source of all I need, then I thrive; then I love and love well. "God is Love," a phrase from scripture (1 John 4:7), can be seen on billboards, signs, books, and songs, verified by all who have chosen to follow Him.

Recently, I read the suggestion to replace the word "Love" in 1 Corinthians chapter thirteen with the name, "Jesus." I testify to the statement "God is Love." I testify to every "Love" or "Jesus" statement above. My faith in Him has given me a centering and grounding in Love, and His Love is my ultimate source. Therefore, love provides: patience, gentleness, kindness, rejoicing (joy), humility (self-control), slow to anger (peace), honesty and forbearance (goodness), and a safe place (faithfulness). All of these are the attributes of God, who is Love, and love provides.

References:

Scripture quotation marked TPT is from The Passion Translation®. Copyright © 2017, 2018, 2020 by Passion & Fire Ministries, Inc. Used by permission. All rights reserved. ThePassionTranslation.com.

M.A. FULTS

Born into an Army family, and with thirty-nine years serving in and then working for the US Navy, Fults spent many years traveling and living in foreign countries, including four years in Tehran, Iran.

She holds a BFA in Drama Production from the University of Arizona and an MS in Management from the Naval Postgraduate School in Monterey, CA. After retiring for the second time in 2022, Fults continued her lifelong pursuit of learning while embarking on her newfound passion for heart healing, financial advising, and life coaching. She has been blessed with one son.

Book Series Website: *www.TheBookOfFrequency.com*

MARANDA CARLILE

TUNED TO LOVE: WHAT I ALMOST MISSED

A STORY OF MARRIAGE, MISALIGNMENT, & AND THE POWER OF GRATITUDE

I stood in our laundry room, clutching a basket of unfolded clothes, too exhausted to cry, too overwhelmed to keep going. Grad school. A full-time job. Kids who needed a more present mother. A marriage slipping through my fingers.

I hadn't slept more than four hours in a row in days, but it wasn't the exhaustion that undid me. It was what I saw out of the corner of my eye.

He had made dinner, folded the towels, wrangled the kids, and was now quietly wiping down the counters like it was no big deal, as if holding it all together came naturally. No complaints. No expectation. Just steady hands doing the work of love in silence.

That's when it hit me: I'd been so focused on what was missing that I couldn't see what had been there all along.

I used to think love looked like late-night conversations and matching spiritual routines; that love came wrapped in deep talks, passionate alignment, and big gestures. That it would feel obvious, poetic, and easy to name.

And when my marriage didn't look like that, I wondered if it was broken.

I stacked us against old stories, expected him to meet unrealistic ideals, meet standards shaped by our religious upbringing, and judged myself by a version of womanhood I thought I was supposed to embody.

You see, I came into adulthood with a nervous system wired for survival. My childhood was unstable. My parents fought, divorced, remarried, and divorced again. My mom's mental and physical health consumed our lives and shaped our home. We struggled financially. The house was always a mess. I didn't always feel wanted, even when I was loved.

While I carried some beautiful, messy memories, I also carried this: People leave. Things fall apart. And I better brace for it.

When I met my husband, I craved safety, but didn't know how to receive it. He was calm and steady, funny and kind, the most loyal person I'd ever met. When I was overwhelmed, short-tempered, or too tightly wound, he had a way of disarming me, not with advice, but with humor. He could make me laugh when I was stuck in seriousness, soften me when I was too rigid. In the beginning, that steadiness felt like solid ground beneath my feet.

But over the years, my gratitude for that steadiness, what once brought me peace, began to stir frustration.I started to long for more, for him to initiate family prayers, to lead in spiritual ways, to share in rituals the way I imagined devoted couples did. I craved depth. I wanted to dream together, to talk through building stability and creating a life we could both feel proud of.

Money had always been a stressor for me. Growing up, things were tight and unpredictable, and I carried a deep desire to create security. That drive made me resourceful and calculated, often working multiple jobs just to feel a sense of control.

Let me take you back to another moment that marked a turning point for us that set our beginnings.

When we were dating, he had aspirations of becoming a dentist. In my mind, that meant stability, security, something predictable. After we got married, he completed an internship at a dental office as he prepared to take the Dental Admissions Test (DAT) before applying to dental school. He came home from one day and said, "That's not the path for me. I want to be a firefighter."

I froze.

It felt like everything I had counted on, financial stability, safety, the plan, had just been pulled out from under me.

Not only was firefighting a complete pivot from what I'd envisioned, but September 11th, 2001 had just happened a month before. Hundreds of firefighters had died that day while on the job. And now my new husband wanted to run into burning buildings for a living?

I told him I couldn't support it.

Part of it was fear. The thought of him running toward danger made me sick, but the other part? It was financial. I couldn't see how that profession could support our family. I had grown up watching money disappear as fast as it came in, and I was determined to not repeat that cycle.

So, I said no, I didn't want him to do that. Not because I didn't believe in him, but because I was scared and I wanted guaranteed stability.

He didn't pursue firefighting at the time. Not because he changed his mind, but because I asked him not to.

Looking back, I see what a sacrifice that was. At the time, I thought I was protecting our future. But in truth, I was trying to control it, grasping for something predictable in a world that felt anything but.

He stayed in a job he didn't really love, trying to find his way, carrying the quiet weight of dreams he'd set aside for me.

And still, he showed up in so many ways, he went to work every day at a job he didn't love, mowed the lawn, fixed the cars, took out the trash, and kept our household laughing.

But slowly, I started to resent him for what I thought he wasn't doing.

I stopped seeing who he truly was to me.

We almost lost each other because of that.

By year fourteen of our marriage, we were both quietly making plans to walk away. We were in therapy. We weren't connecting. I was knee-deep in comparison and unmet expectations. He felt like he was always failing me. I felt like I was always carrying everything.

Then grad school hit, and I couldn't do it all anymore. Working full-time, raising kids, and pushing through clinicals left me stretched thin. I was chasing stability, climbing toward a future I thought would finally feel secure.

I had no choice; I had to start letting go. The "glass balls" I was juggling started to drop, and he stepped in, quietly, steadily, like he always had.

He took over the cooking, the shopping, the kids, and the calendar. Not perfectly, but wholeheartedly.

And as I sat through lectures on pharmacology and pathophysiology, something else began to shift, not in him, but in me.

I started seeing him again.

And I began to see what had been there all along.

I saw the little things: The way he'd pick up my favorite snacks without asking. The way he always made sure my car had gas. The way he joked with the kids just to keep their spirits up. The way he never once complained, even though his own career goals were on pause so I could chase mine.
He hadn't stopped loving me. I had just stopped noticing.

Gratitude is a funny thing. It doesn't erase the hard stuff. It's not a filter to cover what's not working. It's a lens that brings what is working into focus. It's the frequency that tunes your heart to the truth.

And the truth was that I was married to a good man who had been showing up all along.

The more I leaned into that truth, the more I fell in love again —not with some ideal, not with a fantasy version of him I had been waiting for, not the version the world told me I needed, but with the man in front of me.

The more I noticed what he did do, the less I obsessed over what he didn't. The more I thanked him, the more I found things to be thankful for. The more I dropped the script, the more love had room to grow.

We still have hard days. Sometimes my old patterns whisper that I need more. That I'm too much. That I'm not truly seen.

But those voices have quieted, because now I know what love actually feels like. It feels like safety, like socks on the floor over which I no longer trip emotionally. Love feels like a man who always has my back, even when I don't have my best face forward.

Love, real love, is quiet and fierce. It's not performance. It's presence—and gratitude is how I stay connected to it.

THE FREQUENCY THAT SAVED US

Do you want to know the frequency that saved our marriage? It wasn't just communication. It wasn't counseling. It wasn't romance.

It was recognition. I started seeing again, and once I saw, I couldn't unsee. I saw the man who stayed, the man who steadied our home, the man who taught our children joy, the man who never told me no and always supported my aspirations and dreams, even when I couldn't do the same for him. I saw the man who loved me when I wasn't very lovable.

I stopped measuring love in words and devotion to appearances or expectations and started measuring it in energy. In time. In effort. In the little kindnesses. In the million things that go unseen until you choose to see them.

WHAT I'D TELL HER NOW

If I could sit with the younger version of myself, the woman who felt let down, lonely, and unsure whether her marriage was worth saving, I'd gently take her hand and say: Stop measuring love by how it looks and start feeling for how it shows up. Love isn't always poetic. Sometimes it takes out the trash. Sometimes it's quiet and tired, but still present. Don't miss it because it didn't come with flowers.

Drop the script. Drop what people tell you how it should be.

The world may tell you how a partner should act, pray, speak, or love. But what if love isn't a checklist? What if it's a frequency, and you've just been tuned to the wrong channel? Let people love you their way.

Your partner may not be as expressive as you are. They may not love with words, but they may express their love through time, loyalty, or service. They might not share your spiritual beliefs anymore, or perhaps your spiritual languages have shifted, causing you to stop speaking the same faith-based dialect on which your marriage was founded. That used to feel like a deal-breaker to me.

I kept measuring him against the image of the spiritual partner I thought I was supposed to have, the one who would lead with conviction, initiate prayer, and be the guiding force in our shared faith. And because he didn't fit that picture, I questioned his devotion, our foundation, and whether we were truly aligned.

But over time, I realized something deeper: Who he is matters more than who I was told he should be. Spirituality doesn't have to look the same to be sacred. We stopped speaking the same religious language, but he never stopped showing up in the ways that mattered most. He kept showing up with loyalty, protection, steadiness, and service. And I never stopped being loved, even when his beliefs shifted and his practices no longer mirrored mine.

Gratitude is not a personality trait; it's a practice.

You don't feel grateful and then see beauty. You start looking for beauty, and gratitude follows. Start by noticing the little things. Love expands where it's recognized.

Control is not connection. Releasing control doesn't mean lowering standards. It means raising your awareness.

Your nervous system doesn't always tell the truth. Just because you feel unsafe or uncertain doesn't mean you're unloved. Sometimes, the fear is old, and the love is now. Learn the difference.

This work, this tuning in, this surrender, this gratitude, it didn't just restore my marriage. It refined me. It softened the edges that trauma hardened. It taught me that strength isn't about control, but rather about compassion. It showed me that healing isn't just about fixing symptoms. It's about learning to see clearly.

It rewired the part of me that was always waiting for the other shoe to drop. It anchored me in love, not just with my husband, but with myself.

This frequency, the frequency of love and gratitude, is what guides me now as a mother, a wife, and an integrative medicine practitioner.

Because healing isn't just about labs and protocols. It's about helping men and women feel safe, seen, and whole, sometimes for the first time.

Your invitation: Tune in today. What are you missing because it doesn't look like what you expected?

If you're still searching for love, connection, or safety, maybe it's not missing. Maybe it's just been waiting for you to slow down, soften, and truly see.

Take a breath. Shift your focus. And tune in again.

Because what you almost missed... might be the very thing that saves you.

MARANDA CARLILE

Maranda Carlile, FNP-BC, is a board-certified Family Nurse Practitioner, TEDx speaker, international presenter, and founder of Astra Health and Wellness. She helps high-performing women and men rebalance hormones, heal the gut, restore energy, and reclaim their health through a personalized, root-cause approach. She serves as a cohort leader for the BHRT Academy, is recognized for her expertise in functional lab interpretation and gut health, and brings over fourteen years of trauma-informed care experience as a Sexual Assault Nurse Examiner (SANE). Blending science with deep empathy, Maranda understands how being dismissed when something feels off can affect your ability to show up—for yourself, your family, your relationships, and your career. She believes you deserve answers that go deeper than surface-level labs or symptom suppression. As a wife and mother of three, Maranda knows the power of showing up fully—for yourself and those you love. Whether on stage or in the clinic, her mission is to take a comprehensive, whole-body approach to help you feel safe, seen, and whole again—through advanced lab testing, hormone optimization, and gut healing.

Author's Website: *www.AstraHealthAndWellness.com*

Book Series Website: *www.TheBookOfFrequency.com*

MARIS SEGAL & KEN ASHBY

LOVE & GRATITUDE: LIFE'S POWER FREQUENCIES

Life is never a straight path. Like music, life can be a driving loud rhythm, or flow easily like cool jazz. In our twenty-plus years together, we have experienced life from one spectrum to the other. There have been joyful twists and turns, unexpected detours, and moments of trauma and drama that created doubt and made us question just about everything. Through all of it— the triumphs and struggles, we are lovers of life and each other!

Love and gratitude have been among the foundational cornerstones and primary notes of our individual lives and are central to our journey together as a couple, steeped in family and as business partners. We wake up in the morning and choose each other every day, beginning with our gratitude and meditation practice. This sets a grounding rhythm and tone as we greet new possibilities and navigate challenges.

Love and gratitude also shape how we serve others as transformational business leadership coaches, and especially how we relate and lead in our personal and professional lives.

The concept of "frequency" is often used to describe our emotional state. Love and gratitude influence the "frequencies" of both our emotional and mental states, which are considered mindset and heart-set. When we love with respect and practice gratitude, we shift into a higher, more fulfilling way of living. Imagine a room filled with music. If the music is chaotic and loud, it can create stress, whereas if the music is calm, uplifting, and rhythmic, it can create peace. Love and gratitude work in the same way—they influence the "music" of our emotions, guiding us toward harmony and positivity in our minds.

Imagine that you have a radio inside of you that plays all kinds of music and frequencies. When you're frustrated or upset, the music might sound gloomy or loud. When you feel love— when someone gives you a big hug or tells you they care—the music shifts to something warm with a groove—gentle, rhythmic, and happy.

Now let's look at gratitude. Think of it as turning up the volume on your favorite songs. When you stop and think, "Wow, I'm blessed to have my friends, my family, my health, my work, and all the fun-filled moments in my life." It's like tuning the radio to a brighter, more joyful station and feeling lighter, happier, and more connected to the world. When that happens, people around you also shift. Love and gratitude allow us to be in high-vibe energy and shift frequencies!

LOVE ROOTED IN RESPECT

Love is the ultimate connection between people, whether in friendships, family, or romantic relationships. But love without respect is incomplete. Love first begins inside each of us with respecting ourselves. Love breeds kindness and is about honoring who an individual is, valuing their thoughts, and giving them the space to be heard and grow.

Can love and gratitude be applied to business? Yes! In our coaching, we are honored to work with businesses that are evolving into a more people-first culture, driven by heart-led leaders, who are grounded in respect and patience, engagement and acknowledgement, presence and empowerment. That's love and gratitude in business action with bottom-line impact. It's a welcome shift that we hope will keep spreading across the globe!

Maris: Ken and I had known each other for many years, running in the same global cause-related circles and grateful for our shared experiences and friendship. I was living in New York, and Ken was in Colorado. One day, he called to tell me he was coming to New York to launch a national anti-bullying campaign called, *Words Can Heal.* The second he said the name, I literally shivered. "Can you say that again?" I asked, stunned.

Just that morning, I had finished writing the marketing strategy for the very same project, after months of pro bono work. Ken and I had not caught up with each other for nearly a year, so neither of us knew the other was involved. It hadn't even hit the press yet. Little did we know at that moment what would unfold.

At dinner, Ken nervously said, "I'm interested in you." I was surprised… and flattered. My body lit up like a tuning fork. We both felt something shift. We called it "the spark of possibilities."

Across long distances, Ken's heart, music, wisdom, and humor pulled me closer. But there were some obstacles to sort through: Religion: I'm Jewish and always pictured marrying someone who shared my faith. Ken's a Baptist preacher's kid. I'd already had my "practice marriage"—seven years with a Jewish man. Could this be different?

Then there was family—Ken was also divorced, had two grown sons, and had a grandchild on the way. I'd always imagined becoming a mom. Plus, we're fourteen years apart in age. Every conversation was rooted in honesty, curiosity, and respect, which built trust. We kept discovering more about who we were—and who we could be together. What could have been insurmountable, we overcame with gratitude; we honored our differences that became musical notes, creating our connected song as a couple, and our friendship grew into a love story that is still evolving!

Ken: When meeting new friends and clients, we are always asked, "How do you work together without making each other crazy, and still have a personal life?" In fairness, some days we do make each other crazy. However, love, respect, and gratitude are the rhythms and musical notes that keep us in tune! That spark we felt at the beginning still grounds us, and when things feel off, we always come back to it! That's home! We love each other more now than on our wedding day nearly eighteen years ago.

Love and gratitude expand like a sponge, and when shared with others, they cause a ripple of vibrations that uplift all those in connection. I'm not going to lie: We are sitting at the center of one of our most challenging times as a couple, and it is clear to both of us that we are exactly where we are meant to be. We've learned that real love isn't about control or expectation; it's about giving space for others to be seen and valued without conditions. The love we share is grounded in humanity and humility! We bring this to our work every day.

When we love with respect, we create stronger, healthier relationships everywhere in our lives. Love is our source of empowerment and trust versus being possessive or demanding. While a lower frequency can ground in fear and control, a higher frequency evolves connection and mutual appreciation. We always have a choice!

A GRATEFUL HEART SHIFTS EVERYTHING

We stand in gratitude for the impact and accomplishments that we have shared across forty countries and for each person who has been part of each experience, from Heads of State to heads of villages. Of course, we face disappointments, failures, or times when we feel stuck. Gratitude allows us to shift how we see these experiences. Reframing with a lens of gratitude means looking at challenges not as roadblocks but, instead, as lessons and opportunities. "What is this moment teaching us?"

We have learned that when speaking with a family member, friend, or colleague, listening to their perspective offers a reframing of our own view that we may have been attached to. Seeing another perspective offers empowering growth. Gratitude also offers a powerful space of acknowledgement every day for yourself and those around you. We make it a point to offer a simple "thank you" or "job well done," which goes a long way. That's the "grati-vibe" ripple!

Recently, after speaking at an event in California, we had a car accident midday, going about seventy miles per hour. Boom! We side-swiped a car and spun across four lanes of oncoming traffic. In what felt like slow motion, we came to a stop in the middle median facing backwards, and miraculously, we were fine.

We were so grateful that the accident was not worse and that the woman we hit was okay and able to converse with us and the Highway Patrol officer. Even after returning the damaged rental vehicle, we were naturally still shaken. We were also grateful to everyone we worked with that day who held a loving space to support us, even though we were strangers. We could have let that experience overwhelm us with shock, but with gratitude as our grounding, it shifted everything.

Love and gratitude are two of the most powerful feelings in our human relationship experience. They shape the way we see ourselves, how we interact with others, and even the energy we bring into the world. The more we practice them, the more our radio plays the best songs—great rhythms that make us want to dance through life, even through the tough times!

When we choose to lead our lives personally and professionally with love and gratitude, we create a culture of support and belonging. We inspire others to see beauty in their own lives and the lives of others. If there's one thing we know for certain, it's this: The way we move through the world and how we relate matters. We believe that the next evolution in our human story is mastering connected relationships with love and gratitude at the core. How are you tuning in to love and gratitude?

Download our Grati-vibe guide for a daily gratitude practice at *www.SegalLeadershipGlobal.com.*

MARIS SEGAL & KEN ASHBY

From Mindset to Marketing, Ken Ashby and Maris Segal, a husband and wife dynamic duo, have spent the last thirty-plus years bringing an innovative, collaborative voice to issues, causes, and brands. As entrepreneurs, activists, business strategists, executive producers, coaches, authors, speakers, and trainers, Ken and Maris work with the public and private sectors from boardrooms and classrooms to the world stage. Their leadership expertise in Business Relationship Marketing, Organizational Change and Cultural Inclusion, Personal Growth, Project Management, Public Affairs, and Philanthropy Strategies has been called upon by companies and their agencies. Their experience includes: consumer and financial brands, Olympic organizers, Super Bowls, America's 400th Anniversary, Harvard Kennedy School, Archdiocese of LA and NY Papal visit planners, the White House, and celebrities across the arts, entertainment, sports, and culinary genres. With Ken's expertise as an award-winning singer-songwriter, they launched ONE SONG, a songwriting workshop series designed to unleash creativity in individuals and teams. Their **DRIVE** method: **D**esire, **R**elationships, **I**ntention, **V**ision and **E**mpowerment sits at the core of their companies Prosody Creative Services, ONE SONG, and Segal Leadership Global.

Author's Website: *www.SegalLeadershipGlobal.com*

Book Series Website: *www.TheBookOfFrequency.com*

DR. MICHELLE MRAS

LOVE YOURSELF TO MIRACLES

How often have you heard, "Love yourself?" I heard those words hundreds of times throughout my life, but really had no idea what they really meant or how to achieve this enlightened level of self-love. The younger version of me would withdraw from the world and wallow in my misery. That wallowing would turn into an onslaught of degrading thoughts of why I was being punished or made to suffer from an outside source. I truly believed my self-pity habit worked well. It did for a good forty-plus years, until it backfired on me.

In May 2014, I was recovering from an automobile accident where I received a traumatic brain injury, or TBI. I was unable to communicate or walk without assistance for over two years. The initial injury seemed minor, but as the days passed, my brain stopped communicating with my body. I didn't realize I was speaking gibberish. In my mind, I heard complete sentences. To those hearing me, I was repeating the words, "Maccaroni, cheese, spaghetti."

Within days, those words left me as well. I was unable to speak more than one fractured word at a time. I was trapped inside myself. A deep depression engulfed me. My inner critics emerged with a full assault, highlighting all my failures and my inability to succeed. It was unbearable. The saving grace from my suicidal thoughts was that I couldn't move to act upon my plan.

With no way of expressing my thoughts, I spent over two years alone in my mind. My old coping mechanism of self-imposed exile was no longer by choice. Forced isolation and wallowing backfired on me. I hated not being able to leave it. I remember the day that I prayed and begged God, "Kill me." I shared this event in my 2016 TEDx Talk in more detail, but I heard a response from a booming disembodied voice telling me, "You're not dead, yet!"

While the words were being said to me, I saw a movie flash in my mind of every painful experience from my lifetime. In each frame, I saw something very large and transparent protecting me from something much worse. I believe I saw my Guardian Angel. I can honestly tell you that when you hear a voice from everywhere at once, you pay attention. That was when my condition began to serve me. Instead of being angry for my isolation, I began to explore the magic of being alive. My comfort zone of retreating and berating became a time to reflect on my past lessons and evaluate how to shift my mindset from what I lacked to what I could do.

Instead of crying when my inner critic berated me, I began to challenge the thoughts. I realized that in my catatonic state, I could observe those around me without notice. I registered body language and voice intonation, and relished the musicality of the various voices from people around me and on television. This major turning point led to a significant shift in my mindset, which subsequently accelerated my healing process.

For the majority of my life, I didn't feel worthy of love. There was always something not petite, smart, pretty, or pure enough, etc. As my attitude shifted, my healing was directly proportional to positivity. The tiny mental shifts I experienced opened my willingness to seek therapies to regain my balance, heal my brain, and, in turn, my soul. I began to truly believe that I was possibly worthy of life, love, and of achieving my wildest dreams. Most of all, I began to learn how to like, accept, and see value in my perceived flaws.

This wasn't a quick shift. It was more of a slow knob turn to the right. My healing was not linear. Nothing worthwhile is easy. I would make progress, overdo my new ability, and fall back over and over again. The miracle was in my understanding that each setback was temporary. There were many moments where my husband just held me as I cried from exasperation. Healing was a long, slow, uphill climb.

You would think, throughout all the self-discovery and healing I was working through, that I would have experienced a massive enlightenment. I kept hoping for a Blues Brothers' moment, where I'm in church screaming, "I see the light." I didn't. I didn't realize I made much progress until I recognized that my self-loathing was irrational. That one act of clarity was a huge step, but I had difficulty maneuvering through those feelings.

So, instead of forcing myself to see my worth, I turned to my husband, Michael. He has loved me since we were high school sweethearts. I asked him to tell me what he saw in me and why he loved such a broken person. I took note of all that he shared about the woman he saw in me. I immediately began to consciously embody those traits he knew to be inherent in me. I borrowed his belief and love for me because I didn't have enough on my own. I held what he expressed close to my heart and would turn to his list whenever I felt unworthy. It has taken years of living within his love to finally believe and love myself.

During this journey of self-discovery and shift to self-love, I realized a practice of gratitude for my very existence was essential. Without consistent daily gratefulness check-ins, one negative comment or experience would send me sliding back down the slippery slope to self-loathing and feelings of inadequacy. Every morning, I do a quick, grateful call out for: Waking up, all the body parts working to move me, my blurry vision, etc… Strangers ask me why I am always smiling. Others ask if I am putting on an act for the outside world. What I share is that I'm grateful for the gift of life! Every day above ground or free of excruciating pain is a great day.

I've had numerous epiphanies on my journey. Each lesson has served me well. One in particular, which I believe is the cornerstone of my resilience, is that "Miracles occur when we love ourselves." My automobile accident affected me for years. Almost ten years later, I still experience TBI symptoms, which cause me to adjust how and when I perform tasks. These three lessons have served me well throughout my mental and physical healing journey: One, love thyself; two, gratitude for everything; and three, higher consciousness—there is more that we can't see.

These lessons opened my path to the opportunities and manifestations that occurred along the way. During the second year of my recovery from my TBI, when I only had a sixteen-second memory, I was invited to, auditioned for, and landed my first TEDx Talk. Immediately afterward, multiple doors of opportunity opened, which manifested as accolades and awards that came to me. I became a well-traveled inspirational speaker within two years of learning to walk and talk again.

My trajectory has been direct and fast as an internationally recognized speaker, coach, trainer, and author. Now, I am also highly sought after as a gala singer in addition to being the keynote speaker. None of these opportunities would have happened if I hadn't embraced and loved the person I am, including my flaws.

My earlier quote needs a slight modification: "Miracles occur when we love ourselves completely." I'm living proof. Through sharing my experiences, I guide my clients and audience members to examine themselves. We must learn to see the beauty within our flaws. Our perceived flaws are where our biggest gifts to humanity hide.

My challenge to you is to have a deep look at yourself. When you reach an aspect you wish to avoid, that is where you need to dive deeper. Purpose and determination are in those dark places. Once you find your true purpose, you will discover how to express yourself completely. In that magic experience, love yourself through acceptance of the magic that is you.

Living within our purpose, we find the fuel to keep moving in joy, light, and love. The miracle of truly loving yourself is the catalyst to manifestation.

DR. MICHELLE MRAS

Dr. Michelle Mras is an award-winning global and TEDx keynote speaker, executive speaking coach, international bestselling author, 20x Amazon bestselling author, and co-author of thirty books. Michelle is the host of the MentalShift show on *The New Channel (TNC)* in the Philippines, and co-host of the Denim and Pearls podcast. She has speaking parts in several sci-fi movies; check *IMDB.com* for her. Her music EP album can be found on *MichelleMras.com*. Dr. Michelle was nominated for the Most Influential Filipina in the World and is a United Nations Ambassador for Peace.

Dr. Michelle Mras is a survivor of multiple life challenges, including a traumatic brain injury, breast cancer, and human trafficking. Dr. Michelle is a proud military daughter and spouse who has traveled and lived around the world. She uses her vast experience to guide her clients to recognize the innate gifts within them, to stop apologizing for what they are not and step into who they truly are. Dr. Michelle's driving thought is that every day is a gift. Tomorrow is never promised. Every moment is an opportunity to be the best version of you... Unapologetically!

Author's Website: *www.MichelleMras.com*

Book Series Website: *www.TheBookOfFrequency.com*

MR. WHISKEY

BENDING TIME WITH LOVE

"So, Jacob labored seven years to get Rachel, but they seemed like mere days to him because of his love for her."
~ Genesis 29:20 NIV

There are countless quotes and songs about love that I could reference to represent myself, but none do it so well as the one above. Not only does it summarize my personality and life story well, but it's also a great example of the many applications and definitions of frequency. In this particular case, we'll be focusing on frequency as a concept of movement through life at a certain speed, or perceived speed, as well as a state of energy and being.

Most commonly, time moves at one speed, but our perception of it can be skewed to seem faster or slower. An hour adventuring with your best friend and an hour in traffic can both feel like drastically different experiences, despite the same amount of time having passed.

I could list countless factors that affect our perception of time, but the one we'll focus on is love. It's actually one of the most powerful forces that can change our perception of time. We all know the saying about how time flies when you're having fun, and I believe that time flies even faster when you're in love. Of course, love is different for everyone and changes throughout our lives, but one thing is universally certain: The frequency of love is powerful.

Sometimes, love can be blinding. It can cause us to become obsessed, break our morals, change our lives, and sometimes, everything about ourselves. Some people will go to drastic lengths for love—and I'm one of those people. That's how I realized the frequency of love can be powerful, but also something to be cautious about.

Balancing love is already a difficult task, but when you add being a Nuclear Operator in the Navy to it, love becomes exceedingly more complicated. There's rarely free time. If there is, it's pick one thing—sleep, hobbies, socializing, love, errands—and then it's back to work. The rest will have to wait for another free moment, if it comes at all.

Now, there's a way to get more free time and do more than one thing: give up your sleep. With multiple coffees or energy drinks a day, military members are known for being caffeine addicts. I, however, did not partake in that—*love* was my caffeine in the military instead.

There have been many "she's the one" moments and devastating heartbreaks in my life. I've been on countless dates, and I've foolishly fallen in love with many women. Due to my traumatic upbringing and my parents' severely skewed views of the world, I didn't understand love. I didn't grow up witnessing love in a healthy way. In fact, I was told I'd spend my life alone and die unloved.

The military made love even more complicated, but unlike high school, I had some success. This is when I first tapped into the frequency of love.

It started with giving up sleep. Love fueled me through sleepless nights and long shifts. However, it was nothing compared to when I was truly in love with my (at the time) fiancée. That love was far different from what I had experienced prior to meeting her. Our first date lasted fourteen hours, and I had driven over two hours to see her, and then two more to return home. She had almost refused to meet me, wary of having me drive "so far" to see her for the first time. Little did we know that the drive I made that day would seem like nothing compared to what was to come.

As the mission often calls us to do, I had to move away. By that time, I had fallen deeply in love. So, what now? We were separated by quite the distance, after all. In turn, my weekend lifestyle became a testimony to my love—the labor I would do as Jacob did for Rachel.

My weekend schedule became this: I'd work most of Friday. Then, I'd immediately drive over eight hours to see my then-fiancée. Saturday, I'd spend the day with her before sleeping for a few hours. Then, I'd wake up and spend Sunday with her before driving overnight—eight hours straight—to the ship, where I would then work several hours. If it was Duty Day, that became a twenty-four-hour shift, often with overnight duties that same evening.

Truly, I couldn't do that drive again—not without love. I say that because I drove that route a few times again for my friends, and it was unbearable. The first time I drove back to see them, all I could wonder was how I had ever done it several times a month without hesitation, failure, or complaint.

That was when I realized how powerful the frequency of love can be. I used to make that drive almost every weekend, and it never felt like anything. I'd go days without sleep, but I was never tired. I'd drive for hours but never question it. Sure, there were days when traffic or other drivers annoyed me—but to see her, it was nothing.

It didn't matter how long the drive was or how casual the date we then went on was, so long as we were together. I'd drive sixteen hours just to watch her do her homework. As we often seek, that love was a place of peace, a different time zone of its own, and I existed in a different state than when without love.

That's the frequency of love.

It's not just romantic love, though. I always emphasize romance, but the frequency of love exists for lifelong friends, between parents and children, and in other relationships as well. So, what can we do with this knowledge?

Shifting our focus to the frequency of love can help make the burdens of life—whether daily tasks or major events—much easier. When you focus on your desire to make the person you love happy and fulfilled, what seems impossible can become possible. The results become more important than the pain of the process.

Love energizes and empowers us—physically, emotionally, spiritually, and mentally—to go beyond our limits. This includes overcoming fear, from major lifestyle changes to small daily anxieties. I moved to a new state, leaving behind all my comfort and familiarity, along with my close friends, to marry a woman. Looking back, I can't believe it. At the time, though, I didn't hesitate for a moment.

Of course, it's important not to let the frequency of your love for someone else override your self-love and self-care. Otherwise, it can be very damaging. Set boundaries for yourself and make time for self-care just as you do for others. Your main frequency of love won't always be there, but a type of it will.

I've been cheated on, lied to, betrayed, used for sex, used for money, used for schemes, made into a sidepiece, left waiting to be married, abandoned, and led on. Yet, I still hope in the idea of love—of finding reciprocated, healthy, and abundant love. Some people call it naïve, and I've often found myself loving unrequitedly, giving everything to people who would not do the same. So, I caution everyone.

However, love can also make anything seem possible. It can make time move in an instant. The frequency of love can elevate your energy and allow you to accomplish what would otherwise be impossible—all while serving others.

So, tell me: How are you going to love? Why are you going to love? Will you control the frequency of love, or will it control you? Together, where will you go, and what will you do? Love wisely, and love strongly, so that your years of labor might seem like days.

MR. WHISKEY

Mr. Whiskey, formerly an Electrician's Mate Nuclear Operator, is a U.S. Navy veteran, podcaster, author, speaker, preacher, comedian, and entrepreneur. As the founder of Couple O' Nukes LLC, he is dedicated to helping individuals improve their lives through global networking, information sharing, and community building—both virtually and in person. Through the Couple O' Nukes podcast and his travels around the world, Mr. Whiskey focuses on mentoring young adults, connecting with outcasts, and empowering passionate dreamers. His mission spans suicide prevention, addiction recovery, fitness, health and wellness, military matters, relationships, parenting, career development, financial literacy, and faith.

When not actively working, Mr. Whiskey can often be found outside with his three-pound Chihuahua, running several miles at a time, writing fiction or poetry, designing women's Kaiju-based fashion, or spending quality time with his elderly neighbors. He also dedicates a significant amount of time to studying the Bible, as well as Hebrew and Greek.

Author's Website: *www.CoupleONukes.com*

Book Series Website: *www.TheBookOfFrequency.com*

NANCY E. MOORE

TUNING INTO MY FREQUENCY

FINDING GRATITUDE IN A SHIFTING WORLD

My life used to revolve around television. It was more than just entertainment; it was structure—a constant. From a young age, I remember studying the TV guide as if it were homework. I would create my schedule for the week. I could understand the TV guide long before most kids my age could understand the concept of reading charts. My sister told me she thought I was a genius because I could read the TV Guide and understand it. It gave me a sense of control and confidence.

Looking back, I realize it was one of my earliest experiences of being in sync with everything. As I grew up, the world moved into the computer era, and everything changed. My timetable was off. The sense of order I felt was beginning to slip away. I did not have any real computer education in primary or secondary school. My careers were customer service-based jobs.

I became a cosmetologist. Guess what? There were no computers for us to work on or even within the cosmetology field. It was great, though—I loved working with customers. However, I started to feel that I was falling behind as the world moved forward. I remember thinking of my grandparents, who went from the horse-and-buggy era to seeing a man land on the moon. The world moved into a technological society, and I was standing still.

Things started to get blurry. I could set aside my checkbook and start tracking everything on my computer, if I had one. I needed to find a place to learn how these things worked. How was I going to keep up with the world?

So, I began my journey. I started by trying to take some classes. I was an okay student; I passed primary and secondary school, so how hard could it be? Oh boy, did I have a lesson to learn. It seems I had been hiding some fun learning issues. When you are a good kid who pays attention in class and stays quiet, teachers often think you are thinking instead of struggling. Many times, the teacher just assumed I was shy instead of realizing I wasn't sure what was going on or what they were asking for.

As I attempted to take classes at the junior college, I finally met an English professor whom I had gotten to know and would touch base with after class to ensure I understood what she was teaching. Then I took the first test. I passed, but only by one or two points. The professor pulled me aside and asked what had happened. I looked at her very inquisitively, wondering what she meant. I asked her for clarification.

She said, "We talked about all of this; you should have gotten a good grade." I looked at her and said, "I passed." She chuckled, and we discussed the test. "Yup," she said, "you know this stuff better than your test grade shows." She decided to send me for special testing. As I met with the RN testing me, we "played games" that are designed to help her see how I see, hear what I hear, and comprehend what I comprehend. It was a crazy eye-opener.

We learned together that I was a visual learner, off the charts at the top, and an auditory learner, off the charts at the bottom. This became important because, growing up, I took tests like these in school; they would average the three test scores together and tell me I was average and that I "just needed to try harder."

I heard that over and over my whole life. I remember wondering, "What does 'harder' mean?" So, armed with this information, I began to look at things differently. I started to give myself a break and understood that my relationship with computers would be complicated. I would always want to know why and have them show me things, but they would respond with a blank screen because I hadn't given them the correct instructions.

These days, I no longer feel "in sync." I can binge an entire season in a night or over a weekend. The anticipation of waiting for Thursday night to watch your favorite show? Gone. The magic of the miniseries—where you had to be home at exactly 8 PM or miss out entirely—has been replaced by an on-demand culture. I sometimes find myself sitting in my car, listening to old-time radio shows, asking, "What day is it? What time is it? What month are we in?" And I'm not lost in the literal sense—I'm lost in the sense of disconnection from something deeper. Something real. It made me reflect: When did I stop being tuned in?

My grandparents used to say, "Things were different in the good old days." I used to roll my eyes at that. But now, I get it. It's not that I long for the past, but it does feel like life moves at warp speed now. Technology keeps evolving, faster and faster, just when I've barely settled into the last change. I finally figured out how to use something, then boom—it's obsolete.

I have changed my point of view. Instead of being overwhelmed, I started shifting my perspective. I began asking myself a better question: What if this constant evolution is a mirror of my own growth? What if the pace of the world is actually inviting me to slow down and tune in—not to the noise, but to myself?

This was the beginning of a real transformation, and I adjusted to the changes in the world. I began practicing gratitude—not just the kind where you make a list before bed (though that's great, too), but deep gratitude. I'd sit in stillness, thankful for the fact that I could remember what it was like to wait for something, that I grew up in a world where patience was learned, and that I experienced the wonder unfolding naturally.

I found my frequency—that inner vibration where joy, meaning, and love live. It's not found in the next gadget or app. It's found in remembering who I am and allowing myself to appreciate the journey.

When I look back, there is so much change. Music lived on vinyl, became 8-tracks, cassettes, CDs—and back to vinyl again. There's something in that cycle that speaks to the soul. Life isn't linear; it's circular. What we thought we lost often comes back around, sometimes better, sometimes just different —but always with lessons.

I've had to relearn things so many times. When I first got a cell phone, it was like holding the future in my hand. Before that, I remember my grandmother's rotary phone. We were on a party line—you'd pick up the phone, and sometimes someone else would already be on it. I remember phone numbers that started with letters, then area codes. That evolution seems endless, but it's also a powerful reminder: I've adapted to every transition.

There's a quiet kind of love in that—love for the self who figured it out again and again. Love for the little girl who memorized the TV guide. Love for the woman who now helps others navigate their own transformations.

When I tune into that frequency, I feel connected—not to the chaos of the world, but to the essence of life. I feel joy in the smallest things: the crackle of an old radio show, the comfort of a favorite childhood song.

And yes, I still get those moments when someone younger looks at me sideways when I don't understand a new app or trend. But instead of shrinking, I lean in and have them teach me.

There is so much power in memory—not to live in the past, but to draw wisdom from it. And with that wisdom comes our gratitude for what we have. I'm grateful for every evolution I've lived through. I'm grateful for the awkward moments of learning something new, for the joy of rediscovering the old, and for the deep knowing that I am still here—present, learning, loving.

Love, for me, is not just about relationships with others—it's about how I relate to myself. It's in the grace I give myself when I don't "get it" right away. It's in the patience I've learned to extend. It's in the awe I feel when I see how far I've come. Every piece of technology, every shift in how we live, has shown me that I am resilient.

Love fuels the ability to adapt. Gratitude fuels the ability to thrive. So, today, when I feel overwhelmed, I don't hide and think I'm getting old, I breathe.

And I remember to learn, live, and connect.

NANCY E. MOORE

Nancy E. Moore is an Image Strategist and Digital Entrepreneur Coach with over fifteen years of experience transforming personal style into powerful branding across the beauty, television, film, and commercial industries. From working behind the scenes as a makeup artist, educator, and creative director to leading high-profile editorial shoots and ad campaigns, Nancy has mastered the art of visual storytelling and understands how personal image shapes confidence, influence, and opportunity.

Today, she merges her creative flair with digital strategy to guide entrepreneurs in building magnetic, authentic brands that stand out online. As the author of *Style Made Simple: Your Guide to Daily Looks* and the co-founder of a wealth-building company for women, Nancy is passionate about equipping others with the tools to thrive—both in business and in life.

Her signature offering, the Digital Entrepreneur Essentials Package, is a step-by-step framework that helps clients develop a clear and cohesive online presence through brand identity, color analysis, marketing visuals, and strategy—all with a personal touch.

Author's Website: *www.NancyEMoore.com*

Book Series Website: *www.TheBookOfFrequency.com*

NEETU N. PRABHU

I'M STILL HERE: WHAT THEY COULDN'T TAKE FROM ME

THE MIRROR & THE MASK

There was a season in my life when silence became my only language.

Not the peaceful kind. The kind that comes when your nervous system is stuck between survival and surrender. It's frozen, humming, and numb. To the world, I was the picture of strength—an accomplished woman. A mother. A trusted wealth strategist to multi-millionaires across the country.

But behind closed doors, I was trembling. My voice had been stripped from me—literally—by a stroke that left me stuttering and fragmented. My body had been through surgeries, trauma, bruises, and medical reports with headlines that looked like endings.

And my spirit? Some days, it didn't rise at all. Still, I wore the mask. I showed up to client calls with a smile and solutions. I fed my children, told them bedtime stories, sang songs, and made them feel safe. But at night, I curled into silence and shook.

And then came the moment that undid me. One evening, I had a dark skincare mask on—a pathetic, last-ditch attempt at self-care—some overpriced lotion I had smeared on my face, as if that could fix the mess I was hiding underneath. Here's the truth: You can stick all the lotions and potions you want on the outside—but it ain't gonna make you pretty if you're bleeding on the inside.

While I was finishing my skincare routine, my little baby girl walked in. She looked at me, tilted her head, and asked in that innocent, soul-piercing way only children can: "Mama… when are you going to take off that mask?" She meant the one on my face, but I knew what she really meant. And it broke me.

Even in the fire… I was still someone's home. And that someone was watching me closely. She didn't need me to be perfect. She needed me to be real.

So, I made a decision—not out of anger and not to punish her —but from a deeper knowing that whispered to me, "This is not the way your story ends. This is the day you begin again."

After nearly eighteen years of marriage, I ended it. Not to run from pain, but to step into truth. Not to escape this time… but to emerge. It cost me everything I thought I needed. But it gave me back what I didn't even know I had lost.

THE UNRAVELING

People think rock bottom is a single moment. But for me, it was a slow dissolve. Piece by piece.

I had shut down my business—not because I lacked drive, but because my body was falling apart.

I had to choose: Do I serve my family, kids, and clients, or do I fight for my life? I was seeing four doctors a week, and it didn't seem to end. I had an oncologist finalizing my cancer treatment. A neurologist to help me rebuild my speech. A chiropractor to help me walk straight again. A trauma therapist was guiding me through EMDR so I could sleep at night.

People said, "Go back to your parents." "Get a roommate." "Apply for Medicaid." "Take food stamps." They meant well. However, I couldn't accept help because I needed to prove to myself that I could survive.

I had nothing. No income. No business. No stability. Just a broken body, a pile of bills, plus two kids who still believed I could fix anything. And somehow... I kept showing up. Pretending. Smiling. Whispering. Even after the danger was gone, I still took calls in the closet because part of me didn't believe I was safe yet. The trauma was over. But I was still trapped inside it.

THE QUIET RETURN

I started writing. Not because I wanted to, but because I had nowhere else to put the pain. I couldn't talk to anyone—not friends, not family. Not even my therapist. I was drowning in shame, blame, guilt, embarrassment, and silence. But my journal didn't judge me. It let me fall apart. It let me be. And slowly… it let me heal.

There were mornings I wished I didn't wake up. But suicide wasn't an option, because two little hearts needed me to live. So, I did the only thing I knew how to do: I stayed. I breathed. I whispered, "I'm still here."

I sang lullabies at bedtime—the same ones I always had. But this time, I kept singing long after my children had fallen asleep. Those songs weren't just for them. They were holding *me* together. It was my daughter's innocence that kept saving me. Her voice. Her questions. Her presence. She didn't ask for a perfect mother. She just wanted *me*. Safe. Soft. Home.

Gratitude didn't arrive like a sunrise. It came in flickers. Making homemade meals. Writing two lines in my journal. Brushing my girls' hair. Lighting a candle and letting it burn all the way through. At first, I wrote, "thank you," even when I didn't mean it.

Until one day… I did. I wasn't grateful for the pain. I was grateful for the *possibilities* it opened. That I was still here.

That I had survived. That I could write again. Sing again. Pray again. Choose again.

THE RISE

Healing didn't arrive like a breakthrough. It came like a whisper. A small, sacred unraveling. And then… a slow rebuild. Saying "no" without explaining. Sleeping without guilt. Dressing in what felt safe, not stylish. Seeing the woman in the mirror with reverence, not regret. She had survived what should have ended her. And she was still here.

In 2022, I didn't just rebuild—I birthed Unity Wealth Strategies. No ads. No funnels. No website. Not even a social media presence. But clients came, and with them came connections. Clarity. They came to *me* because they could sense something different. They didn't come for marketing; they came for frequency.

In one quarter, I did more business than in the last seven years combined. But more importantly, I made a more profound impact in my clients' lives than ever before.

Because my work? It was never about me. It was always about the difference I was here to make. They didn't just trust the plan; they trusted the presence. Because I didn't just offer a strategy—I offered safety.

I don't chase now. I don't convince. I don't need the world to validate me, because I already chose *me*. And with God on my side, I'm already in the majority. I don't wear stupid masks anymore—I   show up fully. And when I speak, it's from wholeness—not hiding.

Love, to me now, is not a performance. It's a presence. Gratitude is not something I practice; it's the ground I walk on. Every scar, every tear, every tremble… They weren't setbacks. They were seeds. And today, I walk in the very same garden in which those seeds were planted.

MY MESSAGE TO YOU

If you're still sitting in the dark, with a quiet ache in your chest, I want you to know something: You are not broken. You are not too far gone. You are not "too late." You are not "too much" or "not enough." You are not defined by what happened to you. You are revealed by who you choose to become.

I've whispered in closets. I've sobbed into pillows. I've prayed in pieces and sung through panic. But I rose. Not all at once. Not perfectly. But I rose.

And so will you. Just one step at a time; just one day at a time! When you tap into that love and gratitude from within, you JUMP into your Quantum Leap Story! And the best part? The pen is in your hand!

So, if all you can do today is breathe, that's enough. If your voice is still a whisper, keep whispering. Because one day, it will roar. You don't need a plan. You don't need permission.

You just need a mustard seed of knowing: This is not your ending—this is your beginning.

And if you can't yet believe in *you*, borrow my belief. I believe in YOU. And this woman today? If I didn't live the story, go through the flames... even I wouldn't believe it.

And if I didn't know I wrote this, I'd want to find out who did —because this woman? She walks in love, gratitude, and God.

With all my love,
Neetu N. Prabhu

NEETU N. PRABHU

Neetu Prabhu, Founder and CEO of Unity Wealth Strategies, is a distinguished wealth strategist serving ultra-high net worth clients and business owners. She specializes in wealth building, legacy planning, and multigenerational wealth transfers, utilizing tax-free income strategies to revolutionize her clients' financial futures. Neetu is recognized for her fiduciary excellence and ethical service, earning accolades such as the prestigious Million Dollar Round Table Court of the Table award and multiple honors for her impactful decade-long tenure in financial services.

Beyond her professional endeavors, Neetu is passionately committed to empowering single moms and survivors of domestic violence. A philanthropist at heart, she champions financial literacy for women, acting as a guiding force to foster independence and resilience. She is also a multi-time #1 Amazon Bestselling Author and a featured speaker alongside notable figures like Brian Tracy and Erik Swanson.

Author's Website: *www.LinkedIn.com/in/NeetuPrabhu*

Book Series Website: *www.TheBookOfFrequency.com*

DR. ONIKA SHIRLEY

ECHOES OF HIS LOVE: A JOURNEY OF GRATITUDE IN ACTION

In the quiet corners of my life, amidst the everyday rush, I've discovered a profound truth: tapping into the frequency of love and gratitude is like unlocking a hidden treasure. It's a radiant energy that vibrates through every interaction, illuminating the paths we walk and the connections we make. This connection to God and to His people has become the heartbeat of my existence, guiding me to recognize the beauty in both the grand gestures and the simplest acts of kindness.

Each day presents an invitation to step into this frequency—a chance to reflect the love I've received and extend it to those around me. From the smile of a stranger to the laughter shared with real friends, I find that gratitude transforms the mundane into something extraordinary. Through my actions, I strive to embody this love, weaving it into the fabric of my community and nurturing the bonds that unite us all. This journey of embodying love and gratitude opens my heart to extraordinary experiences that resonate deeply within, leaving me forever changed and profoundly thankful for the opportunity to make a difference.

"Gratitude unlocks the fullness of life. It turns what we have into enough, and more. It turns denial into acceptance, chaos to order, confusion to clarity. It can turn a meal into a feast, a house into a home, a stranger into a friend."
~ Melody Beattie

At the core of my being lies a profound love for helping others, a calling that transcends mere obligation and resonates with a deep sense of purpose. Each time I lend a hand, offer a listening ear, or provide support in times of need, I am reminded that this love is not just an emotion—it is an active force that has the power to transform lives, including my own. There is an indescribable joy that washes over me when I witness a smile on someone's face, knowing that my actions, however small, have contributed to their happiness or relief.

With each opportunity to serve, my gratitude blossoms. I am thankful for the chance to be a vessel of God's love, to carry His light into the lives of those who may feel lost or burdened. It is in these moments of connection that I see the ripple effect of kindness—how a single act can inspire hope and create a chain reaction of goodwill. The love I have for helping others is intertwined with my gratitude for the privilege of being a part of their stories, accompanying them on their journeys, even if just for a moment.

In this work, I find my own heart expanding, learning lessons of compassion, resilience, and empathy. I am deeply grateful for these sacred moments, as they not only allow me to serve but also enrich my life in ways I could never have imagined. Every time I step forward to help, I embrace the divine purpose behind my journey, celebrating the interconnectedness of our humanity and the boundless love that invites us to uplift one another. Through this sacred exchange, I am continually inspired, constantly reminded that my greatest joy comes from giving love, receiving gratitude, and witnessing the beautiful tapestry of lives interwoven by our shared experiences.

At the age of nineteen, my life took an unexpected turn that would forever shape my understanding of love and gratitude. After two car accidents within a short span of time, I found myself in a place of complete vulnerability. The physical toll was significant, but the emotional and spiritual aftermath felt even heavier. In those moments of pain and uncertainty, as I struggled to regain my footing, I realized that the world can sometimes feel incredibly isolating, even when surrounded by loved ones. My close family rallied around me, offering their support, and I am forever grateful.

It was in the depths of this solitude that I learned to lean on the unwavering love of God. I turned to prayer and reflection, seeking solace in my faith and finding strength in the knowledge that I was never truly alone. God's presence became my anchor, a reminder that even in my darkest hours, I was enveloped in a love that transcended my circumstances. I began to explore the wisdom of scripture, drawing comfort from

THE BOOK OF FREQUENCY

verses that spoke to my heart. Through this process, I discovered that vulnerability is not a sign of weakness, but a pathway to deeper connections both with God and myself.

As I navigated my healing journey, I was struck by the importance of gratitude, even in the midst of hardship. I began keeping a journal, documenting the small victories and moments of joy that arose each day. It was astonishing to observe how the simple act of focusing on gratitude began to shift my perspective. Instead of dwelling solely on the accidents and the challenges they presented, I began to celebrate my resilience, my family's dedication, and the support that came from those who genuinely cared for me.

In quiet moments of reflection, I found that my experience could empower others who might face their own struggles. I started sharing my story, motivating people to embrace their journeys and reminding them of the beauty that can emerge from even the most difficult situations.

Through this transformative experience, I learned that leaning on God's love breeds strength and resilience. The moments when I felt alone were often the very moments that deepened my faith and gratitude. I began to understand that our pain can serve a purpose—when we open our hearts to the lessons they teach us, we become vessels of love ourselves, able to uplift and support others in their times of need. Every prayer, every grateful thought, reinforced my conviction to not only heal but also to help others heal and thrive. From that point on, I committed myself to serve—a living testament to the enduring power of love, support, and gratitude that had carried me through my darkest days.

Here are three lessons I learned, with a relevant scripture passage for deeper self-reflection:

Lesson 1: Embrace Vulnerability as Strength: It's okay to feel vulnerable. Acknowledging your feelings and circumstances is not a sign of weakness but a pathway to personal growth. In my darkest moments, I found strength not by suppressing my vulnerability, but by leaning into it and allowing God's love to fill those empty spaces.

"But he said to me, 'My grace is sufficient for you, for my power is made perfect in weakness.' Therefore, I will boast all the more gladly about my weaknesses, so that Christ's power may rest on me."
~ 2 Corinthians 12:9

Lesson 2: Cultivate a Heart of Gratitude: Gratitude has the power to transform your perspective, even during challenging times. Keeping a gratitude journal helped me focus on the positives in my life, which in turn lifted my spirit and fostered hope. Recognizing the blessings in disguise can help you see the silver lining in any situation.

"Give thanks in all circumstances; for this is the will of God in Christ Jesus for you."
~ 1 Thessalonians 5:18

Lesson 3: Lean on God for Comfort and Purpose: In times of distress, draw near to God. Your relationship with Him can provide you with the peace and purpose needed to navigate life's challenges. Trusting in His plan allows you to find comfort amidst uncertainty and empowers you to inspire others through your experience.

"Cast all your anxiety on him because he cares for you."
~ 1 Peter 5:7

These lessons not only encourage personal growth and resilience but also invite you to seek solace and strength in your faith, reminding you that you're not alone in your struggles.

DR. ONIKA L. SHIRLEY

Dr. Onika L. Shirley is the Founder and CEO of Action Speaks Volume, Inc. She is a Procrastination Strategist and Behavior Change Expert renowned for helping individuals build unshakable confidence, overcome procrastination, and transform dreams into reality. A Master Storyteller and International Speaker, Dr. O serves in Global Ministry and is an international bestselling author, multiple award recipient, serial entrepreneur, and global philanthropist who has impacted lives in the USA, Africa, India, and Pakistan.

As a Motivational Speaker and Christian Counselor, Dr. Onika is dedicated to making a positive difference. Her accolades include being recognized as an Exemplary Global Leader and a Woman of Excellence by I Change Nations, receiving the Passion Purpose Peace Award, and the Presidential Lifetime Achievement Award.

With a heart full of purpose, Dr. O continues to walk in service, striving to make a lasting impact on the lives of others.

Author's Website: *www.ActionSpeaksVolumes.com*

Book Series Website: *www.TheBookOfFrequency.com*

PAM KURT

RESET YOUR MINDSET THROUGH LOVE & GRATITUDE

"We can either complain because rose bushes have thorns, or rejoice because thorn bushes have roses."
~ **Abraham Lincoln**

I am writing this chapter post-COVID, which caused a "reset" for the world. During the pandemic, there were many changes. Perspectives shifted as our "norms" regarding business, problem-solving, and everyday life evolved. This period allowed many people to pause and reflect on what truly matters.

Well, I was one of those "people." My business and personal life were always busy and successful. I had the mindset to get things done and do the best I could for others. I worked a lot—I still do, honestly. But I forgot about gratitude and those simple moments. Sometimes, when you're in the daily grind, you set goals, achieve, and repeat. We do what we are "supposed" to do and expect. *But…* where is our true mindset?

For me, COVID allowed me to get back to basics. I reset my mindset. I know that, for me, it's about gratitude, my faith, and daily practice of positivity. I feel like I was going through life busy, and busy, even busier. I reached goals and was "thankful" for reaching them, but I still felt empty. COVID allowed for the quiet, still time. The time to reflect; the time to be grateful for little things, big things, time to ponder, and just be.

As things pick back up to "normal" speed, I don't want to forget to get back to basics. I want to be grateful and still take time to simply be. I think my best times are when it's quiet. "Be still and know" is one of my favorite scriptures to date!

When you are still, reflect. Do you love yourself? Would you treat others the way you treat yourself? Would you put the limits or the to-do tasks on others? Would you have the same expectations? There is a difference between pushing yourself to reach goals and condemning yourself because you didn't finish your daily "to-do" list. Give yourself the same grace and acceptance you do others. Love yourself. And for this be grateful!

How do you reset your mindset? How do we maintain that reset? Some of the best practices include daily gratitude and reflection, time to be, self-care, and maintaining a positive outlook.

Start to view negatives as a chance to learn something (positive). A "lesson or blessing" will combat any negativity. Catch your negative thoughts and try to reframe them in a positive light. Don't get me wrong; this takes practice and patience, but it's so worth it.

Sometimes, turning a negative into a positive isn't easy. So, crowd those negative thoughts out by consuming positivity. Don't underestimate the power of a motivational message to shift your mindset to a positive place.

However, shifting to a positive mindset isn't always the best thing right off the bat. When there is a lot of emotion involved, the best thing to do is to allow yourself to feel it. You do yourself a disservice by bypassing your feelings and going straight to a positive affirmation. You have to feel it first in order to heal it. So, have a good cry if you need to. Talk to a friend or a therapist. Once you've allowed yourself to process the emotions, shifting to a positive mindset becomes easier. Be grateful for that moment, and you are on your way to a positive mindset.

The most important step to changing your mindset is to love yourself. Give yourself the same "pep talk" or advice you would give your best friend or family member. If you continue with self-love, your world will change.

Start small. Start daily. Surround yourself with positivity. Think happy thoughts, and you are more than on your way to a reset mindset. You got it!

Loving yourself and feeling grateful will help you be at peace, have a better mindset, and experience more joy. Try it!

Showing love to yourself and being grateful for the challenges and rewards will lead you to the best mindset and the path to becoming the best version of yourself!

Be the best version of you! You deserve it!

PAM KURT

Pamela D. Kurt is an attorney, Bestselling Author, speaker, and certified 10X Business Coach dedicated to empowering women to unlock their fullest potential. With a thriving family law practice and a history of leadership roles and board positions, Pam has always been driven by a passion for helping others. Today, she channels that passion into her business, *Best Version of You, LLC*, where she guides women through personal development, spiritual growth, and business success. A prolific author, Pam has co-authored twelve books and contributed to multiple bestselling series, including *The Everyday Women's Guide* and *Becoming an Unstoppable Woman*. Her works, such as *The Successful Woman's Mindset* and *The Path to the Best You*, have topped charts in categories like Women in Business, Self-Help, and Personal Transformation. Her writing journey, which began as an attorney drafting legal documents, has evolved into a powerful platform for sharing stories of resilience, success, and empowerment. Pam has also been featured in prestigious publications like *Enterprise World*, *Tycoon Magazine*, and *Brainz Magazine*, solidifying her voice as a thought leader in women's empowerment. Connect with her at *pam@bestversionyou.com*.

Author's Website: *www.PamKurt.com*

Book Series Website: *www.TheBookOfFrequency.com*

PATTY SHIH-MEI LEE CAMPBELL

LOVE IS THE HIGHEST VIBRATION

"Perfect love casts out all fear!"
~ 1 John 4:18 NIV

"Greater love hath no man than this, that a man lay down his life for his friends."
~ John 15:13

Love is the highest frequency and form of relational intimacy —when one chooses to put another's needs above oneself. When I first gave birth to my boys, the love that welled up inside of me cannot be compared to any other form of love. Looking into their beautiful, innocent, and helpless faces, I had nothing but pure love. I would do anything for them, and I would protect them completely under my care.

This was also the first realization of the depth of love my parents have for me! It wasn't until I became a mother that I truly understood the unconditional love I am capable of giving to another human being. It is also the humble realization of God's unconditional love for me.

I grew up going to church and have always heard that God loves me. We sing songs of love and adoration to God because He first loved us. I grew up trusting and believing in His love my whole life, and have maintained my childlike faith even though I have also experienced hardships throughout my lifetime.

However, I have also matured in the depth and level of understanding over time. At first, it's an innocent, childlike love that is limited to the egocentric, self-serving kind of love. I give in order to get. If I obey, I get rewarded. When I am nice to others, they are usually nice back to me. I love more for my own benefit than for the benefit of others.

As I matured, I learned to give kindness and love without expectations of reciprocity. I practiced showing love by showing up. I volunteered at church, in hospitals, at schools, and at homeless shelters. I listened patiently to friends who needed to vent or process their thoughts and feelings. People told me that they were impressed by my patience and ability to listen and connect deeply with them. They complimented my ability to accept them, and told me that I made them feel safe to share with me at a deeper level. I studied people carefully and became a master at conflict resolution, peacemaking, and life coaching.

I don't usually say "I love you" to someone if I don't intend to prove it through my actions. It's easy to say, "I love you." It's much harder to follow through with action. Love is a word that has been diluted and used flippantly today, referring even to liking food and inanimate objects. We easily say, "I love pizza!" or "I love your dress and outfit!" We interchange the words love and like as if they're synonymous.

However, there is a vast difference between like and love. Love between husband and wife, parents and children, siblings and friends all involve a commitment of some kind—an exchange and promise of a relationship that is deeper than surface-level acquaintances. This kind of love is tested and tried through good times and bad times. When one is capable of such love, he or she is a keeper and someone to hold on to for the rest of your life.

Unfortunately, not everyone is capable of this deeper love. Even many parents fail to give that kind of love to their children. When we are not shown how to love, we often don't know how to love. This can become a generational cycle of dysfunctional relationships rather than healthy relationships of mutual love and respect. Babies don't come with manuals, and we often parent the same way that we were parented.

When I realized that my parents were not perfect, I decided to study Human Development and take Psychology classes to better understand people. I became an educator and learned to appreciate each precious child entrusted to me in my classroom. I had to decide to keep the good parts of parenting from my parents and improve other parts of parenting that I wanted for my own children. It took years of observing people and practicing relationship skills to become proficient in forming deeper connections with others.

Of course, I don't always show love to my loved ones in the way that they need, and I realize my own limitations and imperfections. Why is it that we often do the things we ought not to, and don't do the things we ought to? Our human nature sometimes self-sabotages and goes against the path that increases our frequency. It takes intentional effort to practice how to love yourself, your family, friends, and beyond. What matters most is our commitment to stay open, receive, and give true, genuine love that the world needs desperately.

I may not be able to reach the world by myself, but I can impact the lives of those around me one person at a time. It's important to me that everyone I have encountered feels safe and accepted by me just the way they are. No judgment. No expectations. Just love.

Gratitude is the result of intentional focus on the good things that we have and are blessed by. When we feel loved, accepted, and safe, we are then able to be thankful for our experiences in this life. Perspective makes a huge difference. The famous analogy of "cup half full" or "cup half empty" comes to mind. In every situation we encounter, we choose how we want to perceive it. We can see it as a terrible curse, or we can see it as a challenge to overcome. We can choose to be angry, or we can choose to be happy. We cannot control what others do to us, but we can control what we do to others. Life is full of harsh lessons and crossroads, where decisions must be made, such as choosing the higher road or succumbing to defeat.

Practicing daily gratitude cultivates deeper and permanent joy. Again, we cannot always control the circumstances that bring us happiness or sadness. However, we can choose how we respond to these circumstances, which results in thankfulness or anger. A positive attitude results in a higher frequency. A negative attitude results in a lower frequency. At what frequency do you want to operate? The choice is yours.

We all are given one body, one brain, and one decision at a time. Are you going to choose to give and receive love? Are you going to focus on the positive? Are you going to exercise your right to choose? Are you going to be mindful and aware of yourself, your thoughts, and your actions? Are you going to own up to your mistakes and ask for forgiveness? Or are you going to make excuses and deflect taking responsibility? Each decision either raises your frequency of love and gratitude or diminishes your capacity to experience life to the fullest. What will you choose today to raise your frequency for tomorrow?

A great life with great relationships is not built in a day. It is built each and every day—one decision at a time. It doesn't matter what cards you've been dealt when you were born. It doesn't matter if you were born into poverty or if your parents got divorced when you were young. No matter what happens to us—and a lot happens to us in this imperfect world—we can overcome and experience victory, joy, and love.

I want to encourage you to take action and make your choices. You will soon find out the consequences of your choices. Based on your choices, you will either experience a higher frequency or a lower frequency. Your life begins and ends with you. May you find the ultimate frequency of unconditional love and joy.

PATTY SHIH-MEI LEE CAMPBELL

Patty Shih-Mei Lee Campbell was born and raised in three different countries with three different cultural experiences. She has learned that there are more ways to be right than just one way. There is so much beauty in each culture, even when they are very different from each other. She is married to a wonderful and supportive husband and has two sons, nineteen years apart. One just turned twelve and the other is thirty-one (and got married this year, May 25, 2025).

Patty loves to connect with people at a deeper level and tackles life with a positive outlook. Although her upbringing and experiences weren't the easiest, she has chosen to stay positive and overcome obstacles with grace and perseverance. Love is her chosen language.

Author's Website: *www.AbundanceGroup.us*

Book Series Website: *www.TheBookOfFrequency.com*

RITU CHOPRA

THE HEART'S SACRED COMPASS

- -

*"The universal flow of energy in love and gratitude is
infinite; there is no end to its reach or depth!"*
~ **Dr. Wayne Dyer**

LIFE IS LOVE OF NATURAL AFFECTION

In the spiritual sense, frequency is often understood as the vibrational energy that underlies all aspects of the universe. Everything in our universe operates at a specific frequency. In spiritual terms, these frequencies affect our energy fields, consciousness, overall well-being, and emotions. Speaking of which, love is the most potent and intense emotion of all.

The idea that everything in existence vibrates at its own frequency is central to many spiritual practices. High-frequency energies are thought to align with higher states of consciousness, love, peace, and wisdom, while lower frequencies may correspond to fear, negativity, or emotional stagnation. These frequencies help restore harmony in the body and mind, connecting us with the cosmic rhythm.

According to spiritual teachings, we attract energies that match our frequency. When our frequency is low, influenced by negative thoughts, emotions, or stress, we tend to attract similar energies. Meditation, gratitude, and mindfulness practice elevate our frequency, which attracts higher-vibrational experiences and people into our lives.

The universal flow of energy in love and gratitude is one of the most profound concepts in spiritual teachings. We are all interconnected by an invisible yet powerful energy current, which manifests as love and appreciation.

LOVE AS THE CORE ENERGY

At the heart of the universal flow is love. This isn't love as we typically experience it in personal relationships, but love is a cosmic force and a fundamental vibration that holds the universe together. In many spiritual traditions, love is the highest energy frequency, the purest and most expansive force. In my native culture, love is expressed in multiple ways across its various languages and traditions. Each word captures a different nuance or type of love, reflecting romantic affection and familial, spiritual, and even divine love. Love is not just an emotion; it is an energetic state.

My understanding of emotional love and love for non-living objects has taught me valuable lessons about emotional growth and spiritual development. When we are in a state of love, we vibrate at a frequency that aligns with the universe's flow. When we experience love, we tap into the universal or cosmic energy that fuels life.

Love embodies acceptance, peace, and unity in its purest form, yet this concept seems complicated to comprehend. Due to its energy of connection to the divine, others, and ourselves, love heals, transforms, and elevates.

Love, whether divine, self-given, or offered by another, has the power to reopen what was shut down not to hurt, but to *reawaken*. It softens the grip of bitterness. It brings light into the shadowed corners. And in time, yes, it stitches torn places with golden threads of grace.

WHERE LOVE BLOOMS, GRATITUDE GROWS

Love without gratitude can drift, but gratitude anchors love in the present, making it luminous and enduring. Together, they form a powerful current: gratitude opens the heart, and love flows through it, creating harmony, healing, and expansion. Aligning with the universal flow of energy in love and gratitude requires a deep surrender. It's about releasing control, trusting the process of life, and allowing yourself to be a conduit for higher frequencies.

Gratitude is the soul's magnet—it draws abundance, peace, and connection. Gratitude is more than an emotion we feel when we receive something; it's a recognition of the inherent abundance and beauty in the universe.

When I truly recognize the good in my life, even the most minor things, it shifts something inside me. It's like my whole energy softens and lifts. That connection deepens every time I pause in gratitude. It's not just a feeling; it's a frequency I tap into and change how I show up in the world.

HOW LOVE & GRATITUDE SHAPED MY LIFE

Love and gratitude are never one-way channels. They circulate. Emitting love and gratitude enriches our lives and contributes to the world's collective energy, but this concept is challenging for many to comprehend.

In love, we are vessels through which love flows back to the world, creating a ripple effect that magnifies the energy. Gratitude acts as an amplifier, boosting the positive energy we send out. Love and gratitude are the keys to a deeper understanding of life's sacredness and the interconnectedness of all things.

My love for nature has been a rewarding experience at various intersections of life, giving me unique lessons, experiences, and shows of its beauty and vibrance. The beauty, colors, fragrance, strength, and moving at its own pace and direction, untamed, mesmerizing, resilient, and robust, so many qualities it carries, and not afraid of shedding it all and re-emerging again.

ALIGNING WITH THE FLOW

Aligning with the universal flow of energy in love and gratitude requires a deep surrender. It's about releasing control, trusting the process of life, and allowing yourself to be a conduit for higher frequencies.

Here are a few ways to practice this alignment:

- **Meditation and Presence**: The more we meditate and cultivate a presence, the more we become attuned to the underlying energy of love and gratitude. In these moments of stillness, we can feel the subtle currents of the universe flowing through us.

- **Practicing Compassion**: Love is most fully realized when we extend it outwardly. Compassion for others, in all their forms, strengthens our connection to the universal flow. It dissolves the illusion of separation and reminds us of our oneness with all life.

- **Gratitude Journaling**: Writing down the things you are grateful for creates a daily practice of recognizing the abundance in your life. This simple act of reflection helps to raise your vibration and opens you to the flow of positive energy.

- **Forgiveness**: Letting go of grudges and resentment frees up space for love and gratitude to flow more freely. Forgiveness releases blockages in our energy, allowing us to reconnect with the universal flow of love.

FROM LONGING TO LUMINOSITY

Longing for love feels like standing in a sunlit room, arms outstretched, with no one to hold. It's the ache behind the smile, the quiet pause after a message that never comes. It stirs in the chest like a tide, pulling you toward someone who has not yet arrived or is lost in time. It's tender, bittersweet, a yearning stitched with hope and shadow. Longing for love isn't a weakness; it's proof you've tasted connection and crave it again, not as fantasy, but as heart-forged touch.

To long for love is to admit you have a heart that still believes in connection, even after disappointment. It's not a flaw; it's evidence that you haven't let bitterness win. Longing means your soul still hopes, still dreams, still reaches. This longing is sacred. It's the echo of something ancient in you, a memory of belonging, of being seen without needing to perform, of being held without having to explain. The inner compass keeps you moving toward tenderness, even if the path is uncertain.

This excerpt from my book, *Mastering Life*, expresses the simple yet intertwined nature of love all around us and the ability to feel, express, and feel joyous: *"To enjoy success, love, happiness, and bounty in life, we must be prepared to accept them and be ready to give love and happiness to others. To be loved, we must learn to love; to enjoy happiness, we must have the peace of mind to feel happiness; otherwise, we risk overlooking these precious gifts of life. Our willpower and determination are two of the vital forces we use to achieve the goals we desire in life. The third and most powerful is love for others and our love for ourselves."*

We must learn to love ourselves and to love all living beings. Find common ground when conflicts and differences exist and accentuate the facts that all can agree on. To love someone, learn to love and respect yourself first. Connect with yourself before you connect with others. Self-love and self-respect boost your confidence and provide the courage to make good things happen.

Love reminds you that you are not too much or not enough; you are exactly the miracle needed in this moment.

"Grace walked beside your jagged edges

and called them sacred.

Gratitude turned your scars into stars,

mapping the sky of your becoming.

Let this be your quiet revolution

To lead with love even when the world forgets!

To extend grace like a hand in the dark!

To say thank you, not just when it's easy,

but when it's hardest to mean it!

Carry these truths not just in your mind,

but in your breath, your touch, your choices.

Let them infuse the way you listen, the way you rise,

the way you rest.

A life lived in love, wrapped in grace,

and rooted in gratitude is the kind of life that changes everything it touches.

You are already the light you seek. "

~ Ritu Chopra

RITU CHOPRA

Ritu Chopra inspires people with her sincerity in coaching and professional leadership experience, which includes managing business and IT operations.

Ritu has solved complex technical challenges in her work with Fortune 500 companies over the past twenty-plus years. Using proven methods and tools, she leverages her management and coaching expertise to bridge IT-business gaps, boost engagement, and empower teams.

As president of Chopra Management Services, Ritu is a creative force, motivational speaker, and certified leadership coach. She is the author of *Art of Life*, *Mastering Life*, *Women Leadership in 21st Century*, and her upcoming title, *Magic in Mindfulness*. As an executive coach, Ritu leads seminars and coaching programs tailored to niche areas, including personal mastery, women in leadership, and mindfulness in daily life.

Ritu brings her passion, humility, and dedication to inspire her clients to engage their heads and hearts in clarity and creation.

Author's Website: *www.RituChopra.com*

Book Series Website: *www.TheBookOfFrequency.com*

DR. *SABRINA PATEL*

LOVE & GRATITUDE: THE BRIDGE BETWEEN WORLDS

Love. It's such a simple word, yet it carries the weight of universes.

Gratitude. Equally unassuming, yet profoundly transformative. As I reflect on my journey, I realize how intricately these two have been woven into the fabric of my life, guiding me through joy and hardship, growth and discomfort, and ultimately, bringing me to a place of peace and purpose.

I was born and raised in Kingston, Jamaica —a place where life has a rhythm, where warmth is as much a part of the people as it is of the sun, and where every greeting feels like family. Our culture is colorful, expressive, and loud in the best ways. Laughter echoes across verandas, and food is always a love language. My childhood was deeply rooted in that Caribbean spirit, rich in community and grounded in resilience.

But life has a way of writing the most unexpected love stories.

Many years later, I found myself standing in the middle of a bustling Indian wedding, wrapped in a traditional outfit, henna on my hands, surrounded by sounds, scents, and traditions vastly different from my own. I had married into a somewhat conservative Indian family, one where customs were carefully preserved, where duty often took precedence over emotion, and where love was spoken in acts of service and familial commitment more than in words or affection. In many ways, it was the polar opposite of what I knew.

At first, the differences were glaring. I came from a culture where I could be bold and outspoken, where individuality was encouraged. Suddenly, I was navigating spaces where silence was respect, where I had to learn to listen more than I spoke, and where tradition wasn't to be questioned but embraced. It was disorienting, at times isolating. I felt like a guest in someone else's life.

But love—real, patient, unconditional love—has a way of breaking down even the most fortified walls.

My husband loved me not in spite of my differences but because of them. He saw my Jamaican fire as passion, not rebellion. He valued my opinions even when they clashed with his upbringing. And I, in turn, grew to see the beauty in his family's values, their deep reverence for elders, their selfless devotion to each other, and their belief in unity above all else.

We were two worlds apart, yet love created a bridge.

And what built the bridge stronger each day was gratitude.

I learned to appreciate the tiny gestures that once went unnoticed; the daily calls from his mother, the careful way his father always asked if I had eaten, even if we had nothing else to talk about. These were expressions of love, deeply embedded in their culture. And they taught me that love doesn't always look the way we expect it to. Sometimes, love is quiet. It's consistent. It's a steady hand, rather than a dramatic gesture.

Gratitude shifted my perspective. It softened my edges. Instead of resisting what was unfamiliar, I began to welcome it. I found comfort in rituals I didn't grow up with. I found joy in cooking foods that weren't my own but became ours. I began to love not just my husband, but also the family, the heritage, and the history he brought with him.

And through it all, I held on to my roots.

Being Jamaican is not something I could ever dilute, nor would I want to. I brought my culture into our marriage, too. Our sons dance to reggae and bhangra alike. Our home smells like curry and jerk seasoning. We celebrate Diwali and Christmas with equal fanfare. Our children are learning that identity doesn't have to be confined to one box. It can be a beautiful blend of many.

To me, this is the power of love and gratitude. Love connects hearts across oceans and cultures. Gratitude allows us to cherish the differences instead of fearing them.

But perhaps the greatest lesson I've learned is that both love and gratitude begin within.

For years, I gave so much of myself to fit in, to adapt, to meet expectations. It wasn't until I turned inward that I realized: I can love others better when I love myself first. I can show gratitude for others when I am grateful for who I am and where I come from.

Self-love isn't selfish, it's essential. It's the foundation on which all other forms of love stand. When I began to truly accept myself, the loud, expressive, passionate Jamaican woman married into a quieter, more reserved Indian world, I found harmony. Not by changing who I was, but by evolving into someone who could honor both parts of her life.

So, to anyone reading this who feels caught between two worlds, who is learning to love across cultures, and who is trying to make space for both tradition and individuality, I see you.

Know that love is not limited by geography or upbringing. It is a universal language that speaks through action, patience, understanding, and presence.

Know that gratitude is the lens that can turn even the hardest moments into opportunities for growth and grace.

And know that your story, your unique blend of past and present, roots and branches, is a gift.

Here are a few takeaways that have anchored me:

1. Love is an action, not just a feeling. It shows up in patience, in effort, and in choosing connection even when it's hard.

2. Gratitude changes everything. When we focus on what we have, we shift from a mindset of lack to one of abundance. And abundance attracts more love.

3. Cultural differences are not barriers; they're bridges. They invite us to learn, to grow, and to expand our understanding of what it means to be human.

4. You can belong to more than one world. Identity is not either/or. It's both/and. You can honor where you came from while embracing where life takes you.

5. Self-love is the soil from which all other love grows. Pour into yourself, and you'll have more to give to others.

Love and gratitude aren't just lofty ideals; they are practices. Daily choices. Small shifts. They are the difference between simply surviving and fully thriving.

Looking back, I never could have imagined that my Jamaican heart would find a home with an Indian family, that two vastly different traditions could become one shared legacy. But that's the magic of love. It doesn't erase differences; it celebrates them. It doesn't ask us to change who we are; it invites us to become more of who we were meant to be.

Today, I live a life rooted in both love and gratitude. And it is my hope that you, too, find the courage to open your heart to the unexpected, the unfamiliar, the beautiful journey of connection.

Because in the end, love isn't just about romance or passion. It's about presence. And gratitude isn't just about saying "thank you." It's about being thankful. It's about seeing the divine in every moment, every person, every breath.

So, love boldly. Be grateful fiercely. And watch your life transform.

Thanks,
Sabrina Patel MD

DR. SABRINA PATEL

Dr. Sabrina Patel is a board-certified family medicine physician and the founder of Zia Health, a concierge functional medicine and wellness clinic based in Ormond Beach, Florida. With advanced training in hormone optimization, root-cause medicine, and functional wellness, Dr. Patel helps patients restore balance, reclaim energy, and align with their healthiest selves. After facing personal health struggles postpartum and being diagnosed with an autoimmune condition, she pivoted from conventional protocols to integrative approaches that transformed her life—and now her patients' lives too.

Born and raised in Kingston, Jamaica, Dr. Patel brings a unique cultural lens to healing, blending evidence-based science with compassion and intuition. She is a devoted wife and mother of two young boys, with a love for baking, the arts, and travel. Through her work, she empowers others to reconnect with their bodies, rediscover their vitality, and live in alignment with their purpose.

Author's Website: *www.SabrinaPatel.com*

Book Series Website: *www.TheBookOfFrequency.com*

STARR COCHRAN
MAGIC, MIRACLES, MANIFESTATIONS

I've lived one of the most amazing, magical lives of anyone I know.

Often, when we're young and busy, we don't think about how circumstances, people, and actions shape the journey we call a lifetime. It is only when either a life-changing event or after decades on this planet that we pause to reflect on the hows and whys.

I've been fortunate enough to have been around for many decades, and I've spent some time recently reflecting on what has made this life so incredible.

For as long as I can remember, I've been able to bring people and things into my life, although it wasn't until later in life that I discovered this ability had a name. I also discovered that many people don't believe they could manifest. Some looked at me like I was some sort of freak; some were curious, and yet others were suspicious.

Before I found fellow manifesters in my immediate circle, my teachers were Dr. Wayne Dyer and Dr. Deepak Chopra. Through their books, I discovered I wasn't alone and what I was experiencing was real.

Along with the lesson of letting go of the outcome and allowing the Universe to work out the details, I believe gratitude fuels manifestations. Being grateful for everything that comes into our lives allows manifestations to continue to happen. And I do mean everything.

I've manifested big things, such as houses and cars, as well as people, and lots of small things. Most days, I can manifest a little magic, like the best parking spot, a coin, an item, or a circumstance that brings me joy.

As I began to notice the frequency of these occurrences, I decided to keep track of them in a "magic, miracles, and manifestations" journal. And as you can imagine, a lot more of all of those started showing up in my life. I express gratitude at the time I experience the event, then again as I write about it in my journal.

My mom was a money magnet. I grew up watching her pick up mostly coins, and I, too, started to enjoy the thrill of finding money. It doesn't matter what it is; each find goes into the money jar, a reminder of daily abundance. Any coin brings a smile, and a dollar bill can bring me to tears. It is because of my sincere gratitude for the small financial blessings that I've experienced larger ones. Over the decades, I've manifested tens of thousands of dollars, which have come into my life out of events and sources I could never have imagined.

Yes, I'm grateful for every penny.

In my younger years, I was a bit of a rebel, drinking, smoking, and sneaking out to meet up with older, felon types. Ah, the naivety of youth. Every so often, my friend and I couldn't get out of the house, and coincidentally, on these occasions, these bad boys were arrested on drug charges. Talk about being grateful for her mom's insomnia! It took a few years and a few close calls, and I was on a better path.

It was good timing because I began to think about becoming a police officer. Hard work, tenacity, and several miracles brought that goal to fruition, and I am grateful every day for that experience. I am grateful to have served my community and for the many lessons I learned about myself and my fellow humans.

I had just finished writing my first book and had no idea how it would get published. At about the same time, I had hired a contractor to complete the interior of my new office space. I don't remember how the topic came up, but as it turned out, he was an author and had just started his own publishing company. His wife was also his editor, and she became mine as well. I was grateful for his initial handholding as I entered this new world.

One of my more memorable gratitude moments from later in life came out of nowhere. I had been married for a very long time, and while it was a good marriage by most standards and definitions, little did I know how deeply unhappy I was. One day, I met a friend of a friend. It was quite an innocuous meeting, really—at first. My hello hug with him enveloped us in such heat it could only have been matched by an Arizona summer sun. I hadn't thought about being with another man since my "I do," and suddenly my body started to respond. What the hell was all that about? I was married. Marriage was a commitment, and I was committed.

But I couldn't stop thinking about him; I couldn't silence the thoughts and feelings that had surfaced. Who knew one hug could have awakened a beast that had been asleep for decades, thought dead, and now wanted out—out of a marriage, out of the wife persona, and out into a life that looked like anything but life as I knew it. I was afraid, excited, and confused, and I couldn't wait to discover what awaited me on the other side.

A friend who met me while I was married described me as a nice, friendly, married woman. Somewhere along the many years of marriage, my personality had taken on the same energy as my married life, which was boring and predictable. Now, he describes me as energetic, full of life, exciting, fun, funny, and most unpredictable.

I am grateful for hugs.

While I've been blessed with the realization of many manifestations in my life, my gratitude attitude is highest when it comes to my health. A recent healthcare professional explained that, even though I may have great genes, my attitude toward life remains the biggest contributor to my extraordinary health. All day, every day, I give gratitude for and love to my most amazing body. No matter what I ask it to do, it rises to the occasion, surprising friends and family and continuing to delight me.

I begin every day with meditation, which includes being grateful for my mental, physical, spiritual, financial, creative, sexual, and humorous self, for everyone who shows up in my life, and for the many messages and blessings that come to me throughout my day. I embrace my angels and guides, who have always had my back, despite the many challenges I've given them.

Sometimes people ask me if I have ever had anything bad happen to me. My answer is a question to them: What is bad? That always gets a curious look. Have "not-so-good-things" happened to me? Of course. However, if you're always coming from a place of gratitude, there is no such thing as bad. There is a lesson. Perhaps a nudge in a new direction. An opportunity.

I get it; life can bring some tough situations, and in the moment, it may be difficult to see anything for which to be grateful. But wait for it. Look for it. It's there. Say "thank you" even when it's hard, and more reasons for an easy "thank you" will appear.

Living a life of positivity and gratitude produces a life brimming with magic, miracles, and manifestations, creating an amazing life. When we live in this space, we begin to see that life is happening *for* us, not *to* us. This shift in perspective doesn't just change how we feel internally; it influences our external world. Unexpected blessings, meaningful connections, and serendipitous events will become part of your life. While abundant and countless, we remain ever grateful.

STARR COCHRAN

Starr became a police officer during a time when women typically became detectives rather than street cops. Seeing herself as a warrior and protector, and acknowledging that she got bored easily, she preferred the street assignments. After serving her community for seven years, she transitioned into the financial sector, where she spent the majority of her professional life. During this period, Starr earned certifications as a Certified Financial Planner, financial advisor, and tax accountant. She also graduated with a business degree and a master's degree in counseling.

Recently, Starr's professional pursuits include writing and public speaking about love, sex, and money at a certain age. After thirty-five years of marriage, she decided that was long enough, and has been single for a while now, which means she has a lot to say about love, sex, and money now that she's at this certain age. Her wisdom will tickle your funny bone and tug at your heart.

Author's Website: *www.StarrCochran.com*

Book Series Website: *www.TheBookOfFrequency.com*

STEPH SHINABERY

ENERGY, LOVE, & THE FREQUENCY OF GRATITUDE

Gratitude has saved my life, and love has brought me back into my body. Frequency is the language my soul speaks, and when I listen, everything changes.

As an anesthesiologist and an intuitive coach specializing in energy work and frequency coaching, I've come to understand that healing begins with how we feel and connect.

I recently found something that's changing my life. It's also changing the lives of others. I've got more clients, I'm doing events, and despite the challenges, I'm still moving forward.

It's all been a wake-up call. I realized—again—that nobody's going to save me. Nobody's going to show up and do this for me. It's time to grow up, stop waiting, and find my way. It was frustrating but also clarifying. If I'm going to do this, I have to jump and fly. And if I fall? I'm fortunate to have people in my life who know me and are willing to walk this path with me. I'm making this up as I go.

And now we're here, talking about something I love: frequency. This is my jam. It's how I live, how I think, how I feel.

Trying to describe frequency in words is hard for me. It's more of a feeling. However, I also understand it on a scientific level. I've studied energy, chakras, grounding, and the way frequency works in nature. When I put my feet on the earth or place my hands on a tree, I know I'm tapping into something real. I don't do it often enough, but I know it changes everything in my body when I do. It's like, "Why don't I do this more often?" I forget what I know.

Recently, I had this powerful encounter with someone at an event. We connected and shared a hug—just a platonic embrace—but something about it was electric. Present. Grounded. I didn't want to leave it. Neither did he. We met again later, and it was still just conversations, just presence. That hug? That was the frequency. That was energy. That was a soul-to-soul connection.

I've been on this journey of letting go of labels—around my identity, my sexuality, all of it. I've entered a space where I feel myself as an energetic body. When I work with clients, I show them this model of three concentric circles. The innermost circle is the divine—God's source, spirit, and void. The next is your soul, and the outermost is your body. The body is where all the trauma, stories, and beliefs live. But our souls? They just want to play with each other. They want to connect. And when we can move the body's baggage out of the way, we can experience that soul-level connection.

We are energy flowing, and the energy flows freely when someone is open and grounded rather than guarded. You feel it. That hug I mentioned earlier—that's what it was—just standing there in pure connection. No agenda. Just presence.

And gratitude? Gratitude has saved me more times than I can count. There have been phases of my life where it was the thing that got me through. I can't be anxious, rushed, or angry when I'm in a state of gratitude. Gratitude shifts everything. It's that "thank you" for the simple things: warm coffee, a roof over my head, and kind coworkers.

One time, I came into work and found a handwritten note from a colleague: "I'm so grateful for you. I'm grateful we work together." It was sitting on my keyboard. That moment changed my day.

The more I express gratitude, the more I feel it—and the more it grows. It's like my heart opens, and my energy expands. I've learned to celebrate small wins and pay attention to moments that bring me joy. That shifts my frequency. And it doesn't have to be complicated: I might wake up thinking, "Ugh, I thought it was Saturday." But then I catch myself: "My bed is comfy. I've got a good job. I'm not on call tomorrow." That kind of reframing changes my body.

I've also experienced love as a frequency through somatic healing. I had a session recently where the practitioner barely touched me—just held my head gently, moved slowly, and mindfully. I was fully clothed, and yet, my nervous system relaxed in a profound way. There is no sensuality, just sacred space. His calm, divine masculine presence allowed me to move and release energy. That's love. I try to do that for others when I hold space for them. I'm not fixing them—I'm just present with them, loving them as humans and energy bodies.

Love, gratitude, frequency—they all merge. They're not separate. They're different, yes, but they're deeply tied together. When I'm talking about this, I feel it in my body. I can love myself, flaws and all. I can love my life, even if it's not perfect. And I know everything is unfolding perfectly, divinely, as it's meant to.

And there's this everyday kind of magic, too. I don't always have a big transformational story, but countless micro-moments. For example, I got frustrated when driving home from work and getting stuck in traffic. But now I catch myself.

I take a different route and explore a neighborhood I've never seen, and suddenly, the irritation becomes curiosity. I shift from rushing to noticing. That's presence. That's gratitude. That's frequency. I'll turn on music or a podcast and just enjoy the ride. I think that's what it all comes down to—being present with what is.

Write this Down:

"When I choose gratitude, I shift my frequency. When I lead with love, I allow connection. My presence is power."

So that's my practice. Love and gratitude are not just ideas but living frequencies, just as the pulse of life itself.

When I tap into that presence and choose it intentionally, everything changes. And when I forget? I forgive myself, and I return. That's the path. That's the frequency of love; when we choose it, we don't just survive. We begin to radiate.

STEPH SHINABERY

Steph Shinabery is The World's Best Possibility Coach, a Nurse Anesthesiologist, Artist, Speaker, and the Founder of Genius Code Academy.

After spending much of her life in a career that lacked the inspiration and fulfillment she knew was available to her, she began a journey to answer the question: "What is it I truly desire?"

Her journey led to the creation of the Genius Identity Code™, a process for unlocking your gift, purpose, and path, and helping people see, believe, and execute their unique genius to achieve miraculous outcomes.

Steph works with creative experts, entrepreneurs, and coaches to help them embrace their authenticity and create a life that gets them excited to jump out of bed every day!

You can find her talk, "Wake Up Your Genius Machine," on Amazon Prime Video's *Speak Up: Empower Your Ideas, Season 4.*

Author's Website: *www.StephShinabery.com*

Book Series Website: *www.TheBookOfFrequency.com*

TYLER WATSON

DON'T JUST HAVE GRATITUDE —GET AN ATTITUDE

Let's make something clear right from the start: Gratitude without alignment can keep you stuck.

I know that's a pretty unusual thing to say in a book about the power of gratitude.

Gratitude has been shown over centuries of human practice and decades of scientific research to be one of the most powerful things we can do to feel better, live happier, and create abundance in all areas of our experience.

So why, then, are so many supposedly grateful people not really happy or abundant? I believe that it all comes down to definitions.

When most people use the word "gratitude," they are actually thinking about the cliches society taught them as children, such as,

- From yourself and others: "You shouldn't want more; you should be grateful for what you have," or, "Be grateful you have food/clothes/shelter, there are starving children in _____ (some other place)."
- From caregivers and teachers: "After all I've done for you, the least you can do is be grateful."

In each of these situations, the message is clear: wanting something more is wrong, or we are wrong for not catering to the needs of other people.

Because of this, many people learned that the word "gratitude" means "to pretend to be happy about situations in your life that you don't actually like."

We've been told to just be grateful, and, on the surface, that sounds noble. But underneath it? Gratitude has become a modern excuse for staying in situations we don't want, tolerating income that's not enough, and emotionally pacifying lives that aren't even close to ideal. After all, we tell ourselves, "It could be worse."

I've seen people get addicted to the idea that their struggle is sacred. They call it being humble and thinking positive. They wrap it in a nice little gratitude blanket that says, "Well, I'm just thankful to be here."

But behind that gratitude? A silent scream. A knowing that what they're accepting is not aligned.

And the kicker? That version of "thankfulness" is what actually keeps them trapped.

I remember the moment I knew my gratitude was working against me. I was a massage therapist, charging less than $15 a session. I had forty-nine cents in my bank account. No savings. No strategy. No idea what to do next.

But I was "thankful." Thankful to have a roof. Thankful for food. Thankful I had clients—barely. But if I'm being real? That gratitude was a mask. I was using it to avoid owning the fact that I was playing small. Inside, I knew I wanted something totally different. Because I thought I needed to be grateful, I tried to keep myself "happy" with where I was at. My thoughts, emotions, and my body were trained to settle for my current life. Yet, I was completely out of alignment with what I truly wanted.

When scientists, philosophers, and scriptures tout the benefits of gratitude, they are talking about something completely different.

True gratitude is a doorway to freedom, not the status quo. It gives you power, not excuses.

To me, real gratitude is acknowledging that everything in life is a gift, from our body to this beautiful planet. We did nothing to earn either this life or the world on which we live, yet every day, the sun rises, lungs continue to breathe, and hearts beat.

Because life is a gift, we have a duty to make the very best of it we possibly can.

So, right now, I want to guide you through an exercise that helped me go from pretending to be happy as a broke massage therapist in the name of being "thankful," to making millions of dollars living a life I'm insanely passionate about. A big part of that shift was learning to redefine words I was taught by the limited culture I grew up in, so that they actually mean what I want them to mean.

Our thoughts shape the stories and scripts we use to create our lives. Our words and definitions, in turn, shape our thoughts. If we constantly go through life telling ourselves to be grateful for what we have, when in our minds this actually means "pretend to be happy when life sucks," we are spending an awful lot of time lying to ourselves and other people.

So, here is what to do about it. I teach my clients a process called Redefining Definitions.

Step 1: Pick a word that is important to you or that you want to create more of in your life. In this case, we will do Gratitude.

Step 2: List all of the negative or non-ideal definitions and experiences you have of that word. Include things other people have said and the ways it was used as a weapon against you. Be honest. There is no point in continuing to lie to yourself. If you think you don't have any negative definitions of Gratitude, go deeper. Keep writing until they are all out.

Step 3: Now, on a new sheet of paper, write your ideal definition of Gratitude. What do you want it to mean? What positive emotions do you want it to evoke? What experiences do you want to have because of Gratitude? Be thorough and tell yourself the truth about what you really want.

Step 4: Get rid of the old definition and embody the new. When I work with clients, I use a simple body-based process called "Aligning" to shift the way every cell in their being interprets the word, creating a lasting change. The whole process is outside the scope of this book, but I'd love to share it with you. See the link in my bio at the end of this chapter.

Redefining definitions is one of many powerful steps in transformation. The next steps can totally change how you see the world and the results you experience every day. I can't wait for you to experience them.

If you're still holding on to things that don't serve you but telling yourself to be "thankful" for them, here's your wake-up call.

You don't need more affirmations. You need a frequency upgrade. It's not about being positive. It's about being honest. It's about getting your cells to say, "Yes!" to what's actually true.

Gratitude without alignment isn't gratitude. It's resignation. If you're stuck in the same relationship pattern, the same income plateau, or the same health issue—and you've been "grateful" the whole time—it might be time to tell the truth.

So, here's the new mantra: Don't just have gratitude—get an attitude.

I'm not here to tell you to stop being thankful—I'm here to help you stop settling in disguise.

Your soul knows when something's off. Your body knows when something's real—and your frequency knows when it's time to rise.

So don't settle. Don't sugarcoat. Don't spiritualize being stuck. Honor what's good.

Then *align* with what's true.

You weren't born to cope. You were born to create.

Empowered gratitude doesn't keep you where you are—it pushes you into who you are really meant to be.

TYLER WATSON

Tyler Watson is a speaker, transformational coach, and creator of the Cellular Alignment Technique, a breakthrough method that aligns your body and frequency to your deepest truth. After struggling for years with survival patterns masked by "positive thinking," Tyler discovered how to unlock real change—not just in the mind, but at the cellular level.

Today, he helps leaders, entrepreneurs, and high performers shift beyond coping and into powerful creation, freedom, and flow. Tyler is passionate about teaching people how to stop settling, align their frequency with what they truly desire, and live their ideal lives faster than they ever thought possible.

Learn how to align your body and frequency to your full potential with Tyler's free gift here: *www.AlignmentEffect.com/More*

Author's Website: *www.TylerJWatson.com*
Book Series Website: *www.TheBookOfFrequency.com*

VICKI PARKER

SACRED TIME, SIMPLE MOMENTS: THE POWER OF SHOWING UP

"Let us be grateful to the people who make us happy; they are the charming gardeners who make our souls blossom."
~ **Marcel Proust**

Love carries a frequency. It hums beneath words, pulses through time zones, and travels farther than miles ever could. We may not always speak it out loud or show it every day, but it's present—alive in our gestures, glances, and efforts to stay close, even across distance.

Gratitude gives that love shape and presence. When we are truly grateful, love flows more freely, more often, and with deeper resonance. That sacred pairing—love with gratitude—has become the foundation of my life and the relationships I cherish most.

A JOURNEY OF FAMILY, FRIENDSHIP, & THE FEMININE HEART

I've been blessed with an abundance of people to love. And while I'm deeply grateful for the number, it's not the quantity but the quality that fills my spirit.

As someone who traveled more than 250 days a year, I made presence my priority. I'd drive hours for a meal, a hug, or an evening chat. My besties, Chris and Frankie in New York City, know this well. I once made a two-hour commute each way just so we could laugh together. These are quiet affirmations of love and gratitude.

My college friend, Alycia, once called me passionate about the people in my life. She's right, I am. My Uncle Bob lovingly calls me the "spark plug" of our family, not because I'm loud, but because I bring energy, connection, and consistency.

That consistency sustains the frequency of love. You don't need to see someone every week to feel close. It's the energy you bring. It's the joy, care, and gratitude that keep love alive.

I carry deep gratitude for my family. My mother, one of nine siblings, is still with us and continues to radiate love and grace. From her, I inherited the blessing of twenty-five first cousins and four brothers, and the example of loving generously, staying connected, and leading with kindness.

In recent years, several of my cousins, including Cathy, Hayley, Penny, Heidi, Ruthanna, and I, have created intentional moments together. We celebrated our sixtieth birthdays with a trip to Las Vegas, met in Connecticut for a spa weekend, went to Vegas again to see Cher in concert, and this year reunited at Thurby, a uniquely Kentucky celebration. These gatherings have become a sacred rhythm, providing us spaces to realign, remember, and rejoice.

Together, we've created something beautifully intentional: a space to celebrate, mourn, and revel in our family's love.

What I treasure most isn't how often we're together—it's the energy we bring. Whether a planned trip or a spontaneous call, it's the intention—the love and gratitude infused—that matters.

This extends beyond family. My friendships with women like Kimberly, Hope, Kate, April, and Sue have deepened through our desire to remember who we are, reclaim our divine feminine power, and walk more closely with Source. We speak of softening into confidence, welcoming care, and embracing the strength in being seen. These spirit-rooted sisterhoods remind me we are never alone.

Old friends, like Peggy, Karen, and Julie, have found new life through one message, one invitation. Gratitude is a bridge—it pulls us toward one another, invites reconciliation, and fosters authenticity.

One of my most poignant experiences happened just a few weeks ago. My eighty-nine-year-old mom and I traveled to Europe for my nephew's wedding in Lake Garda, Italy. We began in Frankfurt with visits from my cousin George and his family, as well as my co-author and new friend, Michelle. With no hotels booked, because life had been so full recently, and with some health considerations to navigate, it turned into "an adventure" in every sense.

We missed connections, scrambled for restrooms, and spent days flying by the seat of our pants. Yet my mom met every moment with grace. She never complained, didn't hold a grudge, didn't blame the chaos or my lack of prep. She simply flowed. Once, after navigating tight train schedules and a crowded station, I said, "Mom, thank you for your patience." She smiled and said, "I think this is actually very good for me."

That moment settled me. This wasn't "just a vacation." It was sacred time to be fully present with my mom. Even when ordinary, it was extraordinary. That trip deepened our bond, wrapped in humility and grace. I'm overflowing with gratitude for her, the incredible woman I get to call my mom. And, of course, the amazing experiences surrounding Zech's wedding with my brother Joe and his family are priceless!

Some of my favorite connections opened through travel, too—visiting my dad's cousin Kate in Charleston, or dropping in on my Aunt Dolores, simply because I'm passing through. These choices to say yes to connection became transformative moments in all of our lives.

To me, this is the essence of love and gratitude—not in big celebrations or constant meetings, but in everyday moments, quiet intentions, simple gestures, heartfelt presence.

This frequency of love and gratitude whispers across spirit types:

* For nurturers, it offers warmth and belonging.

* For action-takers, it shows up in meaningful living.

* For knowledge-seekers, it teaches that energy multiplied is exponential.

* For blueprints, it builds ritual, trust, and life structure.

MY INVITATION TO YOU

Reach out to five people who matter to you. Let them know how deeply they're valued. Then plan something, big or small, with each of them. A lunch, a phone call, a walk, a prayer. Let your love move through gratitude, and watch how everything shifts.

List your top five here, how you'll connect, and your intention for connection:

_____

_____

_____

_____

AUTHOR NOTES

This chapter reflects how I experience love as a spiritual current, always flowing through gratitude. By sharing these stories, I hope you'll hear your own love frequencies and choose to express gratitude in ways that matter. Whether in celebration or reconnection, know that love, when offered with gratitude, is always enough.

VICKI PARKER

Vicki Parker is a women's empowerment and wellness coach, innkeeper, entrepreneur, and connector of souls. With deep reverence for family and conscious living, she supports women in remembering who they are, reclaiming confidence, and cultivating authentic relationships.

Vicki is a certified NLP practitioner, licensed BANK Trainer and Coach, creator of the Unstoppable Confidence 5-Day Challenge, and an experienced speaker on emotional intelligence, feminine leadership, and frequency-based living. Known by her family as the "spark plug," she travels with intention, presence, and gratitude. She currently resides in the Cuyahoga Valley National Park, where she tends to both souls and spaces with care at The Inn at Brandywine Falls.

Author's Website: *www.VickiParkerUnlimited.com*

Book Series Website: *www.TheBookOfFrequency.com*

WENDY L. CUNNINGHAM BARNES

THE FREQUENCY OF COURAGE

HOW I FOUND THE MEANING THROUGH LOVE, LOSS, & ALIGNMENT

There are moments in life that shift everything. For me, it wasn't just one—it was a series of divine interruptions: love, loss, faith, pain, and, ultimately, the decision to stop surviving and start becoming.

For years, I did what many women do—chased success, crossed off goals, and wore my "togetherness" like a badge of honor. I built a life that looked good from the outside, smiling in pictures, collecting achievements, and checking all the boxes we're told will make us happy. I wore strength like armor, mistaking constant endurance for real living.

But under the polished exterior, I was aching. Not for more things… but for more meaning.

That something more came wrapped in the softest skin and the brightest eyes: My daughter, Paige.

From the moment she entered the world, she changed me. She wasn't just my child; she was my teacher. The kind of love she gave me cracked me open in ways I didn't know were possible. I didn't just want to be a mother—I wanted to become a woman she could look up to and trust with her heart and her future.

I dreamed of everything we would share: dance classes, late-night talks, shopping trips, laughing over inside jokes. I imagined cheering her on at recitals and tucking her into bed after whispering all my hopes for her life.

But life had a different plan.

At just thirteen months old, Paige was diagnosed with pneumococcal meningitis. It attacked her body like a thief in the night, stealing milestones we had celebrated—her first words, her first steps—and replacing them with fear, hospital rooms, and endless prayers.

I remember one night in particular. The hospital was cold and too bright, the steady beeping of machines filling the room like a heartbeat outside us. I sat by her bed, holding her tiny hand, memorizing every curve and crease. Her fingers didn't squeeze me back anymore, but her spirit still filled the room, tangible and alive.

I leaned in close and whispered, *"If all you ever do is breathe, I will still call you a miracle."*

That moment shifted something in me, in the best possible way. I stopped praying for her to be "normal." I stopped bargaining with God for a different outcome. Instead, I began praying for peace, strength, and grace to carry her story well, no matter what it might look like.

And God answered.

Paige lived for fifteen years, and though she never spoke a word after that first year, her spirit spoke volumes. She could communicate with a glance and shift the atmosphere of a room with her smile. Her energy was magnetic and transcendent, like she knew something the rest of us had forgotten.

She became a teacher, not just to me but to everyone who encountered her. She taught patience, presence, and unconditional love without demands or expectations.

And when she passed, the light in my world flickered. The silence was deafening. It wasn't just the absence of her voice or her laughter—the sudden emptiness of a future I had carefully built in my heart. Grieving her wasn't just grieving her physical presence; it was grieving all the dreams I had wrapped up in her life.

But grief, I would learn, is not the end of love. Love doesn't die with the body. It expands. It transcends. It transforms.

And Paige's love? It stayed with me.

In the quiet after her passing, I realized I had a choice: Either let the pain paralyze me or let it position me for something greater. That's when I discovered a truth about frequency I had never understood before.

Every emotion carries energy. Grief vibrates low; guilt, even lower. But love? Gratitude? Faith?

Those are the highest frequencies we can live in.

I realized that if I wanted to survive this loss—and not just survive but grow from it—I had to choose my frequency intentionally. I had to tune my heart like an instrument toward hope, even when everything around me felt broken.

At first, tuning into a higher frequency felt impossible, like trying to hear a whisper through static. The noise of my grief, anger, and exhaustion was so loud. But little by little, as I leaned into prayer, into gratitude, into memory, a clear voice started to break through the noise: purpose.

That purpose became the You Belong Foundation—an organization birthed from Paige's life and love, created to serve families raising children with special needs—families who often feel invisible, unsupported, and left behind. Through our work, we remind them: You are worthy. You are valuable. You belong. Right now, just *as you are.*

I thought that was the pinnacle of the journey. But God wasn't finished with me yet.

Christian, my youngest son, was also born with special needs. He is 110 pounds of pure, radiant joy—the kind of soul who can restore your faith in the goodness of humanity with a single laugh.

But being his full-time caregiver came at a cost I hadn't fully acknowledged. I poured myself out for everyone else, telling myself it was noble and necessary. But slowly, quietly, I was burning out.

One day, during a routine appointment, a therapist looked me dead in the eyes and said, "You need help. You look haggard."

It stung. Deeply. But she wasn't wrong.

I was running on empty, giving from a place of depletion rather than abundance. I was everyone's safe place—but I wasn't safe for myself.

That confrontation became a catalyst. It forced me to face an uncomfortable truth: I cannot serve from an empty cup. I cannot model thriving as a Christian if I am only surviving. So, I chose to heal. Not later. Not when it was convenient. Now.

I began to eat with intention, move with purpose, rest with intention, and pray with intention.

I protected my peace like my life depended on it—because it did.

Self-love stopped being a luxury. It became a sacred necessity.

From that place of healing, a new purpose was born. My husband, James, and I co-authored a book, *The Power of Self-Love for Women*—a guide for women who have lost themselves in caregiving, performance, or pain—a guide for women who are ready to rise.

We taught what we had to live firsthand: How to forgive yourself for all the ways you abandoned your own heart. How to tune your life to the frequency of truth and wholeness.
How to become who you were always meant to be, even after devastation.

Today, every event we host, every coaching session, every Paige Awards ceremony, and every whisper of encouragement through the You Belong Foundation is built on this foundation: Intentional energy.

Because when you're aligned, you attract what is meant for you. When you are grateful, you multiply the goodness already in your hands. When you live in love, you become a force that darkness cannot silence.

And so, I keep becoming.

I become every time I sit across from a grieving mother and offer her not advice, but presence. I become when I share Paige's story and see compassion ignite in another's eyes. I become when I advocate for Christian and every child still waiting to be seen and honored.

Whenever I choose the frequency of courage, love, and truth, I rise again.

That is what courage is. Not a title. Not a platform. Not a roaring applause.

Courage is the quiet, holy decision to show up in love, even when it hurts—especially when it hurts.

Keep showing up. Keep loving. Keep believing.

I now know what I didn't know before: Joy is not the absence of pain—joy is what you choose in the midst of that pain. And when you live from that place, when your heart, body, and spirit are tuned to the frequency of gratitude and love, you don't just survive your story—you become the most powerful, radiant version of yourself inside it. And that, my friend, is the fundamental frequency of courage.

WENDY L. CUNNINGHAM BARNES

Wendy L. Cunningham Barnes is a powerhouse of resilience, faith, and purpose. As a speaker, author, philanthropist, and founder of The You Belong Foundation, she has transformed personal heartbreak into a mission to create healing spaces where hope and belonging take root, especially for families in the special needs community. Inspired by the life and legacy of her daughter Paige, Wendy empowers women to rise into their highest calling with boldness and grace.

She carries a frequency of unshakable love, one that uplifts, heals, and creates room for others to be fully seen. Through storytelling, advocacy, and transformational leadership, Wendy shows that even after deep loss, joy can return, purpose can evolve, and life can be rebuilt with power and compassion. Her journey serves as a poignant reminder that the energy we carry can become a legacy of healing for others.

Author's Website: *www.TheYouBelongFoundation.org*

Book Series Website: *www.TheBookOfFrequency.com*

YURI CHOI

THE FREQUENCY OF LOVE & GRATITUDE

Eight years ago, I stood at the edge of a life I no longer recognized. My father had just passed away from cancer. I had walked away from a secure, well-paying career that looked successful on the outside but felt soul-crushing on the inside. I was unraveling, grieving, and redefining who I was without the titles, roles, or identities I had clung to for so long. Everything I had built was dissolving, and in its place, there was a blank canvas I hadn't yet found the courage to paint on.

Back then, the idea of becoming a coach, an entrepreneur, a published author, or a speaker felt distant. Beautiful, yes. But intimidating. Unreal. Like something reserved for someone braver or more confident than me. Not someone still aching, doubting, and barely catching her breath after life had shattered everything familiar.

But even in the fog of that season—where I was navigating loss, emotional exhaustion, and profound change—I heard a whisper. It didn't come from my mind. It came from somewhere deeper—a place that still remembered who I truly was. My soul, perhaps.

"You can choose to feel now what you're yearning to feel later."

That whisper didn't hand me an easy-to-follow roadmap right away, but it gave me something more powerful: a decision point.

And so, I made a choice. To feel again. To believe again. To begin again.

And this time, I made a choice that it would not come from a place of pushing or proving, which was all I had known until that point. Rather, I made a choice to powerfully design and move towards a vision that I created, grounded in the energy of self-love, love for my purpose in the world, and gratitude for what I knew was waiting for me in my future.

I gave myself permission to dream—and more importantly, to emotionally *embody* those dreams before they ever arrived. They were not just pictures on my vision boards or scribbled goals in a journal. But I consciously chose to practice *feeling* the love and gratitude for my future self then. This was the process of an *emotional rehearsal*: the act of stepping into the frequency of the life I was calling in *before* any external evidence showed up.

I would ask myself: "If everything I desired was already here, how would love feel in my body? How would gratitude move through me?" And then I would sit with that. I'd breathe into it and let it move through me as if it were already true. I did this even when my bank account didn't reflect it fully yet, even when my life still looked like grief, chaos, uncertainty, and even when it felt like a stretch.

I would walk through the world holding the emotional frequency of the future I was committed to:

- Peaceful mornings in a home that felt aligned, peaceful, and inspired.
- Writing books that deeply touched people's hearts and enjoying fully the fulfillment that comes from that.
- Coaching clients who felt like a soul family and feeling into the connection and purpose.
- Speaking to rooms of people lit up from the inside out.
- Being deeply loved and seen for who I truly am.

None of it was visible yet, but I could *feel* it. And in that feeling, I anchored into my future self more and more. This wasn't about bypassing sadness, fear, or loss. I let those feelings have their space, too, but I didn't let them be the dominant leader of my emotional states.

Instead, I began to teach my body how to feel safe in love and gratitude, even in the unknown. And that's when everything began to change. Not everything changed all at once, but gradually, meaningfully, and consistently. In that process, I finally understood that love and gratitude aren't rewards for when life finally "works out." Rather, they are frequencies we can choose to live by *now*. And this was the bridge that opened new timelines. Our personal frequency at which we tune into sends signals to life and the Universe that we trust it, that we're available, and that we're ready.

Have you ever felt excited for a planned trip even weeks or months before it was going to happen? Just like that, with all of our goals and visions, we can allow ourselves to feel the joy in advance because we know it's coming—because there is faith and trust in both who we are and how we are supported by the Universe. Whether it's falling in love, creating a new chapter in your work, finding your soul's purpose, or simply wanting to feel peace, you don't have to wait to feel the love and gratitude you think that version of your life will bring.

You can feel it now. You can practice it now. And that practice becomes the *bridge*.

Today, I wake up in the lush heart of Ubud, Bali. I feel the infinitely radiating love from my heart as the morning light dances through my big windows, birds chirping just outside. I pour myself a cup of delicious coffee, and as the earthy scent rises to meet me, I feel my whole body soften with unconditional love. I feel so grateful. I take a slow breath in.

There's incense in the air as my dog, Rumi, curls beside me. I can feel the warmth from the sun and from the gentle smiles I get to receive every day from the people who live on the island. And in this quiet moment, I smile—because I remember.

I remember the version of me who once cried on her apartment floor, unsure of who she was becoming. I remember the mornings I pretended to feel grateful, just to build the muscle. And now, this is real. Not because everything just happened, but because I *chose* to meet the future me long before she arrived.

The feeling of love? It's not dependent on someone else today. The gratitude? It's not conditional on achievements. It's *here*. In this moment. In my body. Because I've trained it to be.

This is what living in the frequency of love and gratitude does. It changes how you interact with life so that life can meet you there.

And this isn't about fantasy. This is about energetic precision. Frequency is the language of reality, and love and gratitude are two of its most magnetic, expansive, creative forces.

When we live in the emotional habits of the past, we recreate the same patterns.
But when we consistently, bravely practice the feelings of our future, we begin to live them. We start speaking a new language to life, and life responds.

This is why I teach my clients—many of whom are high performers who have lost their connection to joy—to create rituals around this, to lead their lives from energy, not just intellect. To feel rich before the money comes. To feel love before the partner shows up. To feel purpose before the success.

When we anchor into love and gratitude now, we're not just manifesting outcomes.

We're becoming someone new. And that version of us?

They are not waiting somewhere in the future. They are available here and now, through our consciously chosen frequencies every day, if we allow them.

Reflective Journaling Questions:

1. What's one vision I've held in my heart but haven't allowed myself to emotionally experience in advance?

2. If I were already living that version of reality, how would love and gratitude feel in my body today?

3. What small, daily ritual could help me embody those feelings, regardless of what my outer world looks like?

YURI CHOI

Yuri is the Founder and creator of Yuri Choi Coaching. Choi is a performance coach for entrepreneurs and high achievers. She helps them create and stay in a powerful, abundant, unstoppable mindset to achieve their goals by helping them gain clarity and understanding, leverage their emotional states, and create empowering habits and language patterns.

She is a speaker, writer, creator, connector, YouTuber, and the author of Creating Your Own Happiness. Choi is passionate about spreading the messages about meditation, power of intention, and creating a powerful mindset to live a fulfilling life. She is also a Habitude Warrior Conference Speaker and emcee, and she is a designated guest coach for Psych2Go, the largest online mental health magazine and YouTube Channel. Her mission in the world is to inspire people to live leading with L.O.V.E. (which stands for: laughter, oneness, vulnerability, and ease) and to ignite people's souls to live in a world of infinite creative possibilities and abundance.

Author's Website: *www.YuriChoiCoaching.com*
Book Series Website: *www.TheBookOfFrequency.com*

Habitude Warrior Mastermind

Join a team of

AWESOME

Entrepreneurs, Coaches, Business Owners, and Leaders to support you in your journey of success!

Be one of my personal guests for a session!

www.MastermindGuestPass.com

HABITUDE WARRIOR & INTEGRITY PUBLISHING EDITORIAL TEAM

Habitude Warrior International and Integrity Publishing take great pride in our editorial team who put their sweat, tears, and heart into each and every project and national bestseller! Thank you team!

JON KOVACH JR.
Team Manager

Jon Kovach Jr. strives to assist every author and every team member in the process of self-development for ultimate success.

PAT MINTON
VP of Operations

Pat Minton has been with the Habitude Warrior International team for over 20 years getting her start with Brian Tracy & Erik Swanson.

JILLIAN KOVACH
Editorial Manager

Jillian is a vital team member of Habitude Warrior & Integrity Publishing bringing her expertise managing our Editorial Department.

FATIMA HURD
Editorial Team & Photographer

Fatima is our Professional Photographer for Habitude Warrior as well as one of our members on the Proofing Department team.

LAUREN COBB
Editorial Team Member

Lauren Cobb is part of our Proofing Department for Habitude Warrior & Integrity Publishing as well as one of our authors.

To inquire about joining our team please send us an email to Team@HabitudeWarrior.com

LOVE & GRATITUDE

LOVE & GRATITUDE